ASK
YOUR
MOTHER

ASK
YOUR
MOTHER

Family Life and
Other Impossible Situations

THOMAS R. TROWBRIDGE III

WILLIAM MORROW AND COMPANY, INC.

New York

Recognizing the importance of preserving what has been written, it is the policy of William Morrow and Company, Inc., and its imprints and affiliates to have the books it publishes printed on acid-free paper, and we exert our best efforts to that end.

Library of Congress Cataloging-in-Publication

Trowbridge, Thomas R., III
    Ask your mother : family life and other impossible situations /
Thomas R. Trowbridge III.
    p.   cm.
  ISBN 0-688-09019-2
    1. Family—New York (N.Y.)—Miscellanea.   2. New York (N.Y.)—
Social life and customs—Miscellanea.   I. Title.
HQ536.15.N7T76   1990
306.85′09747′1—dc20   90-5403
                                                      CIP

Printed in the United States of America

First Edition

1 2 3 4 5 6 7 8 9 10

BOOK DESIGN BY PAUL CHEVANNES

To Nancy

Honorable mention to
(in alphabetical order)
Annie, Carrie, and Thomas

CONTENTS

INTRODUCTION

ONE winter it started snowing on a Wednesday and didn't stop until late Friday night—the famous blizzard of whatever that year was. Saturday morning was warm and bright. It was a rare day by any standard, but particularly so in New York City. In Central Park, photographers were falling all over each other, hurrying to take advantage of the clean cover of snow as a foreground before it melted or turned black. I got out my wooden cross-country skis, went to the park, and started to ski.

I had a good glide going when an unleashed golden retriever suddenly jumped on the track in front of me. We crashed into each other and I fell, breaking my ski. The dog's owner started screaming at me for hitting her pet. I screamed at her for not having the dog on a leash (that's a violation of §161.05 of the New York City Health Code). As she and I yelled back and forth at each other, a man ran over and said to me: "Buddy, I saw the whole thing. You were right, she was wrong. If you want to sue, I'd be glad to be a witness." It was classic New York.

We both calmed down and I walked home, dragging my one good ski. People I tell this story to usually ask if the golden retriever was hurt. The dog was fine. A few days later I went to a sporting goods store to shop for new skis. It had been years since I had looked at what was on the market and I couldn't believe what I saw. All the skis were made out of materials that ended in "ium," "ite," or "ene" and seemed to be composites of various refinery products. They certainly didn't come from any tree.

Later that day, I thought about the skis, along with other equipment I'd seen in the store and an article about the experience began to form in my head. I wrote it up, worked it over, and sent it to the editor of the Op-Ed page of *The New York Times*. They ran it on Christmas day that year. I don't think many people saw it because my parents bought most of the copies of that particular edition.

After that piece appeared, ideas for others would come to me from time to time, almost always, for some reason, as I walked home from work in the evening. The catalyst was usually a family experience like our only (that's a promise) camping trip or something at work, like the time I lost a button from my suit jacket right before a big meeting. The *Times* published several of my articles and, as I wrote about other experiences, this book began to take shape.

It strikes some people as unusual for a lawyer to do this kind of writing. It shouldn't. In the practice of law, writing is by no means limited to stringing together "whereas" clauses or reciting the obligations of "the party of the first part." Often, for example, we brief issues such as whether the Tax Injunction Act ousts the federal courts of jurisdiction to enjoin enforcement of the anti-pass-through provision of the New York State Gross Receipts Tax on the ground that, under the Supremacy Clause of the U.S. Constitution, it is preempted by regulations promulgated under the Emergency Petroleum Allocation Act. When doing that, not only do you want to be clear and persuasive, you must also find a way to keep the judge from nodding off before page three.

In some cases, putting together the chapters for this book was a similar undertaking. There was the time, for instance, when my wife and I nearly maimed ourselves trying to make sure our son got a good night's sleep before he took the SSAT. At the time, that was no more funny than a Tax Injunction Act issue is inherently entertaining.

This collection begins with the wooden-ski piece and continues with others about experiences that are certainly not unique to our family. I think humor can be found in most situations, whether it is looking for an apartment or children packing for camp. It's even in the standard dinner party but that's more obvious.

ASK
YOUR
MOTHER

Part I

AROUND THE HOUSE

EVER HEAR OF A WOOD SKI?

GROWING up, I often found myself identifying with the people I read about. The progression (compressed) was from Davy Crockett to Holden Caulfield to J. P. Morgan. I recently felt like another character—Rip Van Winkle.

During college in the early sixties, I acquired a lot of sporting equipment. Some of it is giving out, and the replacement process has been a shock. After breaking one of my hickory cross-country skis not long ago, I went shopping for a new pair. The salesman I spoke to said, "We're recommending this laminated fiberglass and aluminum ski, which features hollow polycarbonate tubes imbedded in a phenolic fibroplastic sectioned glass-filled foam core." He thought that was preferable to the one with a polyurethane foam core wet-wrapped with unidirectional fiberglass. When I asked if he had anything in wood, he asked back, "Wood?" He scratched his head and said he'd check. "Hey, Marty!"

he yelled over his shoulder. "Ever hear of a wood ski?" Marty had not.

I bought my sneakers at about the same time as my skis. They were beginning to leave a small trail of canvas threads, so, at the urging of my family, I reluctantly set out to replace them. "Sneakers?" asked the salesman. "Oh, you must mean athletic shoes. Certainly we have them. Will that be for running, jogging, walking, handball, racquetball, basketball, squash, tennis, platform tennis, fitness, or aerobics?" I slipped away when he wasn't looking.

My sturdy wood tennis racquet is still in great shape after twenty years of use. Its strings, however, are beginning to pop, and this spring I thought I'd see what was on the market. At a midtown tennis shop, I was handed a piece of equipment that looked like something one would take, along with its mate, to the Yukon for winter footwear. "Graphite," the salesman explained. "All graphite, with an injected foam core." He also showed me an aluminum racquet and one in composition graphite/fiberglass/epoxy. If I wanted something lighter, he said he could do one in magnesium. I resisted the temptation to ask if he had anything in kryptonite.

My driver cracked this summer, and this seemed like a good time to replace the set of golf clubs I bought twenty-eight years ago. When a salesman offered to show me a new line of metal woods, I asked if his woods came in wood. To be sure he understood me, he queried, "You want a wood wood?" As it turned out, he could accommodate me, but the woods, he advised, came with jade inserts in the clubface. "Jade?" He was dead serious. For the shaft, he recommended titanium over graphite. He was also pushing beryllium copper irons. I can hear it now, as the TV announcer whispers into his mike, "Nicklaus has only a two-foot putt after a booming three-jade and a picture-perfect nine-copper."

I recently read of a new recording of one of my favorite pieces. It was obviously a popular item, and had sold out at the first few places I tried. I finally located it with a call to a nearby store, and asked that the recording be set aside for me. When I arrived, the fellow behind the counter handed me something with the dimensions and heft of a pack of baseball cards. "What's this?" I asked, and was told that it was a compact disc. When I inquired if he had the recording on a record, he curled his lip and said he didn't carry them, adding, "Record? Those big vinyl things that scratch and warp? Why would you want to buy something like that?"

The camera I bought twenty years ago is starting to behave strangely. I don't dare shop for a new one.

TONSILS

My earliest memory is of having my tonsils taken out. I was probably four at the time. I remember the hospital room I was in, the bed I had, and how delighted I was that after the operation ice cream was an important part of my diet. Most of all, though, I remember the tonsils themselves.

My mother, a doctor's daughter, was apparently interested in exploiting the educational potential of the experience. When I woke up from the operation, there was a jar containing my tonsils in a clear liquid sitting on a table across the room. I remember being alternately bored and lonely in that room, and the visits from my friends and family weren't particularly satisfying. Visitors would arrive in groups, and after dropping some candy or a toy on my bed, they'd head straight for my tonsils. Now and then a hand would poke out from the group and wave at me, and I would hear a voice ask how I was doing. After a brief stay, they'd leave, waving backhandedly in my direction while talking intently among themselves about my tonsils. When I left the hospital, I took the tonsils with me.

The operation took place early in my first year at nursery school. I also remember my first day back at school after leaving the hospital. I was no different from any other child who has come into possession of something he wants to show off. On my first day back, I wrapped my little fingers around the jar, took my seat in our car, and was driven to school by my mother. I'm not sure what my classmates thought of me before then. I do know that on that day I was by far the most popular person in the school—possibly the whole town. Girls thought I was terribly brave to have gone through whatever ordeal was involved in getting the tonsils out from inside my body and to be acting as if it were nothing at all. The boys thought the tonsils were deliciously repulsive, and viewed me with the same awe they would reserve for someone who strolled around trailing a dead snake.

There was one exception. I don't remember his name, but early in the school year he had identified me as his enemy. My tonsil-driven popularity made matters worse, and he apparently made up his mind to take me down a peg or two.

Every day at recess, we went outside to play in an asphalt courtyard. On this particular day, as I walked around with my jar in the company of my admiring classmates, my rival seated himself in a pedal car and, pumping for all he was worth, headed straight for me. He hit me, I fell, and the jar arced through the air. It landed and broke with a muffled pop. I still remember my frantic teacher telephoning my mother and asking, "What'll I put them in?" She was told that she could throw them out, which she did.

The next thing I remember is being in love with Miss Morrissey, my third-grade teacher.

STARTING THE FAMILY

FOURTEEN years after my relationship with Miss Morrissey had ended, I met the woman who was to become my wife. It was in Ann Arbor, Michigan, where I found myself sitting next to a snappy blonde as we both registered for law school. Sophisticated easterner that I was, I offered to help her with the registration form if she had any questions. Smiling politely, she said that really wouldn't be necessary. As I was trying to figure out whether each space on the form was for the question above or below it, she got up, handed in her registration, and left the room. Seven years later, we got married.

For two years after we were married, we saw movies, went out to dinner, traveled, entertained, slept regular hours, and saved some money. Then we decided to have a baby.

When Nancy was in her seventh month of pregnancy, we enrolled in a natural-childbirth class. Our teacher was a looker, and quite trim. She seemed even more so against the background of the behemoths in her class. I didn't miss a session. The classes themselves were not for the overly refined. Toward the end of each one, our teacher would tell the women to hike up their skirts and get down on the floor to practice labor and delivery. She taught them to trace circles on their stomachs with their fingers while doing exaggerated breathing in a sequence such as "pant, pant, blow" or "blow, pant, blow." I had my doubts that any set of traced circles or pant-blow combination could deaden the screaming pain these women were in for, but who was I? All the while, the men were supposed to wipe the wife's forehead and give words of encouragement. " 'Atta girl" and "You can do it" were recommended. In what was to be the understatement of the course, the husbands were alerted that, while in labor, their wives might become "ir-ritable."

The finale of each session was simulating the actual de-livery. With their husbands shouting *"Push,"* a roomful of women raised themselves on their elbows and quickly be-came red-faced from the strain. One of our classmates was more reserved. She took notes during the class. When everyone else hit the deck, she would put down her pad and pick up her knitting.

Long after his nine months were up, our son (as he turned out to be) stayed right where he was. It took a day of walk-ing around Chinatown and Little Italy with visiting friends on a steamy Sunday in July to dislodge him. At about 2:00 A.M. the next day, Nancy shook me and said we were going to the hospital. As she calmly zipped shut the overnight bag she'd had ready for weeks, I raced to the closet and fumbled for something to wear. I grabbed a few things, decided against them, and started to put on a suit. I was tying my necktie when I realized it was probably silly to wear a suit to a delivery. I started to take it off, but reconsidered. These things, I'd heard, can take some time, and I might want to go straight to the office. On the other hand, I'd probably want to go home and shower, in which case . . . "We're—running—out—of—time" Nancy called from the front door, where she was holding the elevator. I can't remember what I put on.

At the hospital, they hustled Nancy away and sent me to dress in a sterile outfit. As I was putting it on, someone I recognized from our natural-childbirth class was taking his off. He said he was *really* mad. He had planned to photograph the delivery, and had bought some special high-speed film that would have been perfect. He had cleared it with the hospital and the doctor (he didn't mention getting his wife's sign-off). At some point during the labor, they had decided to deliver the baby by cesarean section. "Typical," he muttered, walking away. "Just typical."

I found Nancy, who by then was well into labor, and asked how she felt. The question was ill-advised. *"How do you think I feel!?"* she screamed, straining to lift her head off the bed so she could get a good look at the idiot. It did not get any better. Over the next few hours, the woman I had proposed to, that gentle bride, the woman I planned to grow old with, barked her commands:

GET THE WASHCLOTH!

I got the washcloth. Fast.

RUB MY BACK. USE YOUR *FIST*! NOT *THERE*!! HIGHER! I SAID *HIGHER*!!

I pointed out that when someone is horizontal, it's not clear which direction is "higher." She was unforgiving.

GET THE ICE PACK! *NOW !!*

As I had suspected, the finger tracings on the stomach and the pant-blow routine weren't much help. Nor did my frequent " 'Atta girl"s or "Hang in there"s improve her disposition. They even seemed to make her madder. To "You can do it," she shot back

HOW DO *YOU* KNOW!!!? *YOU'RE* NOT DOING IT!!!

Had she been able to get her hands on a set of divorce papers, she would have signed them on the spot.

At 6:05 that morning, Nancy gave birth and, with an exhausted smile, was quickly back to normal. By 6:20, the new mother was asleep, and I, with my own smile, went for a long walk.

AT HOME

I always suspected that my father gave me his name so that he would have an excuse, of sorts, to open my mail. I would frequently find envelopes with his handwritten notation. *Oops. Opened by mistake. She sounds like a nice girl. Why don't you have her over some time?* That may be unfair. He doesn't open my mail anymore, and hasn't ever since the blue and pink envelopes gave way to letters with cellophane windows and return addresses of outfits such as Aetna and the Internal Revenue Service.

Our son got the same name.

Thomas came home from the hospital to an adequately sized one-bedroom apartment. The building, however, had no storage space, and everything we owned was in the apartment with us. In the bedroom, one wall was stacked to the ceiling with wedding presents we couldn't use. One gift presented its own set of questions. This was a nice, if slightly chipped, item used to strain tea. It was given to us by a woman known for taking "souvenirs" from other people's houses tucked in a large handbag. As this was common knowledge, people prepared themselves, and it was not a problem. When small children visit, for example, most families put bottles with poisons and breakables out of reach. With this woman, similar precautions were taken with valuables. Someone, though, had obviously neglected to hide the tea strainer. It couldn't be used openly, so it stayed in the shoe box it arrived in. We also had plate cozies, nine candlesnuffers, and more glass pitchers than most restaurants. We didn't know what to do with any of these things, so they remained in our very visible inventory.

In the living room, we had some standard living-room furniture, a dining-room table and chairs, a desk as well as an antique server and a bureau Nancy had bought at an auction. She said that if we ever got a real place, they would fit right in. Nancy spent a fair amount of time at auction views, looking for bargains to furnish the place we might someday have. One evening she reported that she had seen two fire screens that were estimated to go for thirty dollars at an auction the following day. This was too good to pass up, even though our apartment didn't have a fireplace and there was no prospect that we would ever have one that did. Nancy, therefore, planned to go to the auction during her lunch hour and bid on the screens.

She left Wall Street later than planned, and arrived at the auction house to find that the bidding had already started on the fire screens. Anxious and out of breath, she raised her paddle and kept raising it until the screens were hers— at about four times the estimate. By the time she had paid for them, she was late for a meeting with a client. As she hurried out of the auction house with the screens, one of them fell, ripping a big hole in one of her shoes before clattering to the pavement, where the impact broke off its brass fittings. Once the screen was repaired, it looked fine, as did Nancy's new shoes. Given the substantial investment in the fire screens, they stayed.

Then there was Nancy's palm tree. I hated that thing. It took up space we didn't have, and had to be watered by sitting it in a bathtub full of water. Countless times when I was on a tight schedule, I'd throw back the shower curtain to get at the faucets and discover the palm tree soaking. It, of course, couldn't be moved until it had thoroughly drained, and that took a few hours. I had to learn to adjust my bathing routine so that it didn't conflict with the palm tree's schedule.

One day Nancy was away and had left instructions for me to water the palm tree. I grabbed it by its trunk, slammed it into the tub, and turned on the faucet. Returning to check the water level, I realized that I had turned on the hot water. I say it was unintentional; Nancy insists it was on purpose. By that time, the tub was full of scalding water. I couldn't reach down and pull the plug without burning myself, so there the plant sat until the water cooled. Three days later, it was dead, and we threw it out.

Into all of this, we moved our son and his paraphernalia. His crib went into the bedroom with us, and we put his playpen, changing table, and carriage in the living room. When everything was in place, it looked as though we were getting ready for a tag sale.

We adjusted rather quickly to having to walk around the apartment sideways. The adjustment, however, to the schedule dictated by our son's eating habits was less successful. I have come to think that until people have had to take care of a newborn, they don't know the meaning of the word "fatigue."

It seemed that, for our son, each day was one long meal with several sittings, all of which he attended. There wasn't enough time between feedings for us to get meaningful rest, and taking turns with him didn't accomplish anything. The apartment's configuration was such that when one person was up, everyone was awake.

The first few months of life are a rapid succession of developmental milestones. The newborn starts to make eye contact at close range (8 to 12 inches) in the first month, begins to control his grasp in the second month, can search for the source of sound in the third month, and in the fourth month, can push himself straight up from his stomach. This is what we read. We, however, missed all of that. During those rare moments when we could focus on something other than getting sleep, all we could think about was finding another apartment.

APT. W/WBFPL
AND TURKEY
DEFROSTING ROOM

Our search for a new home was a determined one. Each morning we would turn to the classified section of the paper and read descriptions that set us dreaming wistfully of a new lifestyle. Phrases such as "walk-in closets galore" and "space to spare" did their work, and we'd hurry to make an appointment, praying that the "anxious owner" had not already made his "sacrifice sale" in the "deal of the decade."

We looked for three solid years. In the first apartment we saw, we were attracted by the low price and intrigued by the description "up to three bedrooms." This could be it, we thought; a room for Thomas, one for us, and an extra for guests or to be used as a study. As it turned out, it was really a one-bedroom apartment with a Sheetrock divider in the bedroom. The third bedroom was in the living room, where a corner had been sectioned off, also with Sheetrock. Our own apartment was bigger.

The next one we saw had three legitimate bedrooms. It

was, however, so close to the buildings it looked out on that it seemed to have been lowered into place. I could identify the brand of fabric softener used by the family across the way. When I described this place to a friend and told him the asking price, he said it sounded like a good place to prepare for debtors' prison.

We also saw an apartment that had been vacant for fifteen years. It consisted of a ballroom, one bedroom, and four maids' rooms. I told our agent that we didn't give many balls and that my wife and I doubled as the staff. Never mind, she said. With a bit of work, the place could be made to fit our needs perfectly. The first thing to do would be to convert the apartment to AC current.

One place we saw was a bit outside the area where we'd been looking. The owner told us the neighborhood was wonderful, and assured us that the building was quite safe. They had put barbed wire in front of all the first-floor windows and the block was patrolled, he said, twenty-four hours a day by guards with semi-automatic weapons and Dobermans.

Another building (something like the "Grosvenor" or the "Westminster") advertised "triple mint" apartments "never before lived in." We arrived at the address to find a skeleton of steel girders. As we were about to leave, assuming that the address had been a misprint, we saw a Sales Office sign on a trailer parked next to a cement mixer. Inside, the agent said the apartments would be completed in two weeks and gave us a brochure depicting an elegantly dressed couple alighting from a limousine by a fountain in front of what would be the entrance to the building. When asked to describe the apartments themselves, he could only say that each one would be "a honey."

We finally found an apartment we were both very happy with, and bought it at a time when New York was having a harder time paying its bills than we were. The owner was delighted to unload it, and people thought we were crazy to make such an investment in the city. The place was bigger than we had planned to get, and had rooms we really couldn't use. Like most older New York apartments, it had a full complement of maids' rooms. As we lacked a full complement of maids, these rooms were of limited utility. Shortly after we moved in, a friend came over and was given a tour. Nancy had set out a turkey to thaw in one of the maids' rooms, and our friend dubbed it the "turkey defrosting" room.

I thought the apartment was perfect. Nancy said it needed lots of work. First of all, the wallpaper apparently had to go. We were told that the best way to do this is with a steamer. I rented one, and we started in one of the maids' rooms. The wallpaper came off in no time. So did most of the ceiling. The windows had been painted shut, and the steam emitted by the machine as it chugged away was trapped in the room. The following morning the mist had cleared, and we could see what we'd done. Whatever paint had not fallen to the floor was hanging in thin slabs from the ceiling. The exposed plaster was wet, and, here and there, the paint on the wood trim had blistered. It looked like a set for one of those horror movies in which an unseen force makes everything melt. We removed the wallpaper in the other rooms with a wet sponge and a putty knife.

Then we did the kitchen. I thought it was just fine, but was wrong again. Nancy wanted to renovate it, but she was prepared to negotiate. She said that if I would take charge of getting deliveries of coal for the stove, we could talk.

When the work started, we moved the kitchen operation into the dining room. In went the refrigerator, the toaster oven, a hot plate, and an iron, all hooked up by extension

cords. While the work was being done, we were probably in violation of every fire-code provision applicable to residences. In went boxes and cans of food, brooms, mops, vacuum cleaner, dishes, pots and pans. Everything that is usually tucked away out of sight in a kitchen was sitting either on the floor or on the dining-room table. By then we'd had Carrie, our second child, and her baby gear was in there too. It was a New Yorker cartoon waiting for a caption.

Making matters still more interesting was the footing. The kitchen renovation was to be messy, and so, to protect the rest of the apartment, we covered everything, from the floors up, with big sheets of plastic. If you walked normally on this stuff, by putting a foot out in front and planting a heel, there was no traction, and the foot would slide out from underneath you. We all developed a way of walking around the apartment by taking very short steps on tiptoe. When we were in a hurry, movement was by a series of hops on the balls of the feet, much like an Indian dance. Each time we went outside, we'd find ourselves tiptoeing or hopping on the sidewalk for a short distance until we were sure of our footing again.

With the kitchen done and the wallpaper off, we were ready to start painting. We decided to start with the closets and to paint them white. On my first trip to the paint store, I asked the clerk for a gallon of white paint. He gave me a knowing smile and, without taking his eyes from mine, reached under the counter and handed me a large three-ring binder. It said WHITE on the spine, and inside were at least fifty sheets, each with no fewer than ten different chips. Each of these whites, he told me, was available in a variety of finishes, including flat, eggshell, semigloss, glossy, and high gloss. I did not buy any paint that day.

I began to think I'd live out my days hopping around on plastic, but the work did end. More surprising, once we had spread around our children, furniture, plate cozies, pitchers, fire screens, and the new palm tree, all the rooms were filled up. Now, it's even difficult to find a place to defrost a turkey.

SCIENCE 101

ONE day our son came home from school and announced that his science teacher was accepting requests from students who would like to take Fred, the science-department rabbit, over spring vacation. His teacher wasn't quite sure how he would make a selection among those who wanted the animal—whether it would be first come, first served, raffle, lottery, or a selection based on the teacher's view of the most suitable environment. We told Thomas that we were not interested.

A few days later, he said that his teacher had announced that it was not too late to make a request for the rabbit. Still later and with spring vacation imminent, the report was that the teacher had asked if anyone would be willing to take care of the animal for the two weeks. The day before vacation started, the teacher said that if someone didn't take the rabbit, he wouldn't be able to go on the trip he had planned. Would someone *please* take it? We yielded.

I didn't focus on the rabbit until my wife and the children went to visit her family for a few days, and I was left in charge. The instructions on food and water were very explicit, and I promised to follow them. Suddenly, however, I had to be in Houston one day and in Washington the following morning. Assuming that I would want to go straight from Houston to Washington and spend the night there before my meeting the following morning, my secretary made the arrangements. I, however, was reluctant to leave the rabbit unattended for that long, and could see myself returning to find a dead animal. The damage, however, would extend far beyond the rabbit itself. A son would learn that trust in his father had been misplaced—and his science grade would be put in jeopardy. I therefore booked a 5:00 P.M. plane from Houston, which would get me to New York by 9:00. After getting home and feeding the rabbit, I could be in bed by 11:00, and would have a decent night's sleep before the 7:00 A.M. shuttle to Washington.

I got to the Houston airport in plenty of time, only to learn that the 5:00 P.M. flight had been delayed until 7:00 P.M. That wouldn't be too bad, I thought. I could get home, feed the rabbit, be in bed by one and have four-and-a-half hours' sleep before the shuttle. At the gate next to mine, a flight directly to Washington was about to leave. I considered getting on it, but forced the thought out of my mind and watched as the plane pushed back and left.

Later, the monitors showed 9:00 P.M. as the new departure time for my flight. That wouldn't be too bad, I thought. I could get to New York, feed the rabbit, and be in bed by 3:00 A.M., giving me two-and-a-half hours of sleep before the shuttle. I had managed on less. After one more post-ponement, which would give me just enough time to get to the apartment, feed the rabbit, change, and get back to the airport in time for the shuttle, the flight was canceled. There were no more flights to Washington or New York, but I was able to get on a midnight flight to Baltimore, from which I took a bus to Washington. I arrived at the D.C. bus station at 6:00 A.M. All day long, I worried about the rabbit, but Fred got through the day much better than I did.

That was a few years ago. My wife and I have short memories. Annie, our youngest, asked one day if she could enter the raffle for one of her class science-department's gerbils. She said there was really no reason not to enter the raffle, because the odds against her winning were over-whelming—there were thirty girls in her class and only fifteen gerbils. Every girl, of course, would want one, as they were free. We gave her the go-ahead.

A couple of days later, the odds had changed. Annie knew of at least three girls whose parents wouldn't let them en-ter the raffle. In addition, the number of gerbils had increased by two. As the day of the drawing approached, the chances of our daughter winning one of the animals steadily improved. They improved to the point where, on the day itself, she came home with not one, but two gerbils.

These "free" gerbils (our other children think they are mice), with their $24.95 cages, $6.98 water bottles, $14.95 exercise wheels, and $5.95 bags of food, have taken over the kitchen table. I used to work in there, but all the flat surfaces are now covered by gerbil equipment. I also used to listen to music in the kitchen, but now it is hard to hear over the steady *crunch, crunch* as one animal sharpens his teeth on a toilet-paper roll and *squeak, squeak* as the other one works out on his circular treadmill.

I am looking forward to that point in my children's science education when they start studying things they can't befriend.

THE SSAT

WITH the birth of Annie, our family was at full strength, although Nancy's plaintive noises and wistful looks whenever she sees a newborn often make that less than certain.

They didn't know it at the time, but all three children began taking standardized tests at age three. The first one was the ERB, administered at an unannounced time during nursery school. We knew that our son had been tested when, at the end of the day, he reported that a nice lady with a clipboard had taken him out of class and asked him to play some games while she took notes. His block stacking and peg-and-hole matching abilities were rated, compared with those of children all over the country, and he was put in a percentile.

Standardized tests are given periodically during grade school. Where our daughters go, they try to minimize the anxiety by calling these "bubble tests," so named because the answer is indicated by filling in one circle from a number of choices. The name persisted even after the girls realized that these tests were very serious.

Then came the big one—the SSAT. Our son, being the oldest, took it first, and his performance on this test, taken in the eighth grade, would be a major factor in determining what secondary schools would be open to him. That, in turn, would dictate his choice of colleges, thereby influencing career opportunities, his social life, and his standard of living for the next fifty years. A good night's sleep was the most important (and the only) preparation, so we made sure he was in bed by 10:00 P.M.

A word about our building. It was built in the late twenties, with thick walls that retain heat very well. The heat itself is steam—piped into the basement and then up through radiators in each apartment. The steam is controlled by a timer, and it comes on in ten-minute spurts every hour or so during the day. If the heat were on all the time, the apartments would quickly become stifling, and those short blasts are more than sufficient to keep the building comfortable. At night, the timer turns off the heat entirely between 11:00 P.M. and 6:00 A.M.

At eleven that night, we were getting ready for bed and noticed that heat was still pouring out of the radiators. There was obviously something wrong with the timer, so Nancy, the family expert on heating matters, went downstairs to investigate. In the basement, she fiddled with the timer and came back up. At 11:20, the heat was still on, and our radiator was starting to make a *chuck-chuck pssssss* sound. Back down she went to turn off the steam manually. At midnight, the *chuck-chuck pssssss* continued. The steam valve must have broken, and our apartment was getting very hot.

We were starting to worry. By now, Thomas's room would be like a Turkish bath with noisy pipes, and we wondered if he would be able to sleep. We could sneak into his room and shut the valve on his radiator. That, however, wouldn't be easy, as the radiator valves in our apartment were permanently rusted in the positions they were in when we bought the place. The one in his room was frozen open.

What to do? Do we try to force the valve shut and risk waking him, or do we leave it alone and hope that he'll be able to sleep despite the heat? We could open his window, but the noise from the street would be sure to wake him. We decided to try to stop the heat, banking on his having moved into the REM portion of his sleep.

I carefully opened his door, and Nancy with a flashlight and I with a wrench tiptoed into his room and took positions by his radiator. The radiator itself is enclosed in a wooden cabinet between his bed and the wall. I opened the top of the cabinet and tried to get the wrench tightened onto the valve. The valve is well inside the cabinet and, approaching it at a 60° angle, I struggled to get a good grip. When the wrench was as tight as I could get it, I pushed hard, but the valve wouldn't move. Trying a different approach, I backed off and smacked the end of the wrench with my open palm. The wrench flew off the valve, and ricocheting between the radiator and the inside of the cabinet on its way down, it clattered to the floor. Nancy quickly turned off the flashlight, and the two of us stood quietly in the dark while our son rustled, muttered something unintelligible, and rolled over.

After his breathing returned to a slow, steady rate, we went back to work. To retrieve the wrench, I put one knee on the windowsill, the other carefully on the edge of his bed, and straddling the radiator cabinet, I reached down inside to fish it out. On the first try, my bare arm pressed against the still-steaming radiator. As I yanked it out, I slashed my arm against a sharp edge of the cabinet's tin lining. Throughout all this, Nancy was hissing helpful suggestions such as "Be quiet" and "Be careful."

I eased myself off from on top of the radiator and, holding my arm, slowly left the room to get some protective clothing. Returning with my overcoat and a leather glove, I again mounted the cabinet, and was able to get my hand on the wrench. Inside the overcoat, I was soaked. After several tries, I had a good angle on the valve and it moved. Concerned about snapping it off, I turned the valve as far as I dared, and closed the cabinet cover.

We started to walk out of the room when I heard a shriek—*Reowwww!*—and saw my wife crash to the floor. She had stepped on the cat, who had come to investigate. I froze in place as she lay on the floor and softly moaned. Our son grunted and rearranged his covers.

When the quiet returned, Nancy eased herself up, and I helped her out of the room. We regrouped in the kitchen, where she told me that she had sprained her wrist in the fall. After we had put ice on her wrist and on my burn and I had bandaged my cut, we went to bed. It was 1:30 A.M.

At 3:00 A.M., Nancy got up to check on what we had accomplished. She got back into bed, reporting that heat was still pouring out of the radiator. Thomas was on his own.

In the morning, I went into the kitchen for breakfast, bumping into a few doorjambs on the way. My son was just putting his dishes in the sink, and I looked for signs of the gray scowl that appears on members of our family when they don't get enough sleep. There were none. As he headed out to take the test, I asked how he had slept. "Never better," came the firm response.

ASK YOUR MOTHER

WE read that, after keeping the child warm and dry, parents' primary objective should be to help their children establish good self-images. With low self-esteem, the child becomes a pushover for all of the wrong influences, but with it, he has the self-confidence to do what he knows is right. The child is also much happier. The idea makes sense, as does the advice on what parents should do to make sure their children feel good about themselves.

The literature, however, is silent on another dimension of the question—the effect children have on their parents' self-images. In the beginning, the effect is very positive. When the child learns to talk, he or she masters the question long before the declarative sentence. They come one after another: "What makes the car go?," "Why is the sky blue?," "What makes thunder?" I had all of these, and in each case was able to say, "Come sit on my knee, son, and I'll explain that to you." After the explanation, he would look at me with wonderment, as if asking himself how so much knowledge could possibly reside in one human being.

When the children started going to school, nothing changed—for a while. A daughter would hand me her workbook and ask me to check some homework. The assignment might be one in which she had to circle what didn't belong, on a page that had drawings of a horse, a cow, a goat, and a bulldozer. I would have no difficulty with that, nor would I with most questions about arithmetic and even some algebra. One day, though, my oldest daughter asked how long it would take before two trains passed each other if they were fifteen miles apart and heading toward each other, one at 45 mph and the other at 60 mph. I told her, but she said the teacher would probably want something a little more specific than "Not very long." A recent question, right from seventh-grade math, was to explain the difference between the associative, distributive, and commutative properties of numbers. Questions like this increasingly seem to come when I'm terribly busy and only have time to answer, "Ask your mother." I am always fearful of hearing "She told me to ask you" but that hasn't happened yet.

The parental self-image is not only tested in matters involving schoolwork. In outdoor activities, I notice my children making increasing use of the sentence "Let's wait for Dad." The same progression can be seen in games. Our family plays a fair number of them, such as Chinese checkers and newer games in which you try to get all of your opponents' pieces by trapping them with yours. There's also an elaborate variation of tic-tac-toe. In the early days, I would either win easily or make a stupid move on purpose so the kid could win.

Now, I concentrate for all I'm worth, trying to anticipate all the possible consequences of what I'm about to do. Satisfied that my decision is the right one, I make my move. Often, when I haven't even had time to remove my fingers from the piece, a daughter will give me a puzzled look and ask, "Why did you do *that*?"

Worse, though, is when the game has just started. I have won the toss and make the first move, whereupon the child confidently announces, "You've lost."

One daughter keeps trying to talk me into learning how to play chess, but I have resisted. I don't think it would be too good for my self-esteem.

GETTING FROM A TO B

ONE of the advantages of living in New York City is that you don't have to own a car to get around. Many of our friends keep cars anyway. Among them the talk inevitably turns to the cost of a parking condominium (there apparently is such a thing), the latest antitheft device, and how many radios they have had stolen.

We rent. Renting is the source of different kinds of problems. The first time we planned to leave the city for Christmas, I made my reservation weeks in advance. I arrived at the location on Christmas morning to find an empty garage and a pack of would-be customers leaning over the counter, bellowing at a cowering agent. There were no cars, but some, she promised, were on the way. When pressed for specifics, she said there was a nice Buick Skylark due back from Saratoga that day and a brand new Pontiac Bonneville expected in from Rochester. That made two. There were fifteen of us at the counter. After telephoning my wife to report the situation, I settled in for a long wait. An hour later, a friend walked into the garage. He had learned of our predicament and had come to offer me his car. It was a Porsche.

Somehow, my wife, our son, both daughters, our presents, Christmas cookies, two poinsettias, and I managed to fit into something the manufacturer describes as a two-plus-two seater. As we, hermetically sealed, set out to have Christmas dinner with my parents, I announced that no one was allowed to have seconds.

When we go away for the weekend, the process begins on Friday evening at the rental counter, where an agent will flip through a series of tickets, asking if I want something like a "Daytona," a "Barcelona," or a "Barclay." These names won't mean anything to me, nor will an explanation that a "Barclay" is similar to last year's "Windsor" except that it has about the same amount of leg room as a "Belmont" or a "Surrey" and its trunk is even bigger than the one in a "Tuscany." As in a restaurant, I will usually ask for and go with the house recommendation.

Rental cars are a bit like hotel rooms. With the exception of the most obvious defects, like a missing door, problems don't become apparent until long after anything can be done about them. You don't learn, for example, that the trash compactor is right outside your room and starts compacting every morning at 4:00 A.M. until 4:00 A.M. At one hotel, I went to take a shower before a morning meeting and, as is my practice, I turned on the hot water and soaped up, intending to add cold water when it got too warm. I was fully lathered when I realized that there was no cold water and that the hot only got hotter. I went to that meeting looking a bit pink and smelling very good.

The same goes for rental cars. The "Service Engine Soon" light never goes on while you're still in the garage and nothing lights up to say: "The windshield wipers on this car don't work." Sometimes, though, things work too well. One weekend, we were well on our way when we realized that the heater wouldn't turn off. With all the windows down that July weekend, it was like traveling in a windy sauna.

We, of course, end up with a different car each time. My wife doesn't focus on the make, model, or color, and tends to forget what a particular weekend's vehicle looks like. After grocery shopping, her only sure way of relocating the right car is by identifying the things our children have left in the backseat. I've had the same problem. One dark night, after going to the movies, we returned to what I thought was our car, and I couldn't unlock the door. I struggled with one key, then the other, and finally kicked the door a few times in frustration. It suddenly opened from the inside, revealing two people who were trying to get to know each other better.

The most confusing aspect of renting cars is their nonstandard features. A few weekends ago, I had my first rental of this year's model. I sat in the car and surveyed a dashboard that could not have been less elaborate than the instrument panel on the Stealth bomber. When I turned on the ignition, I heard a steady *wrrrrrrr* as the seat belt automatically closed around me. As we headed out of the city, I stopped at a red light and wanted to make a quick check of something in the trunk. Opening the door and dashing out so as to be back in the car before the light changed, I heard that same *wrrrrrrr* and found my head pinned to the door frame by the sliding seat-belt device. After untangling myself and checking the trunk, I got back in the car, but couldn't get the gearshift back into "drive." Three light changes later, with unsympathetic reactions by those lined up in back of me and some primitive use of the language as they drove by, I finally succeeded. The problem had been my failure to push the SHIFT LOCK OVERRIDE button.

The rest of the trip was uneventful, until I tried to get some gas. The cover to the gas tank was perfectly flush with the side of the car. I couldn't push it in or pull it out, even after clawing at it with my fingernails. There obviously had to be a release somewhere. Inside the car, there was no shortage of buttons and levers. Most of them had little pictures or shorthand descriptions. Some, like ECT NORMAL/POWER, meant absolutely nothing to me. Others I didn't dare touch like the one that said, in red, LIFT FOR EMERGENCY EXIT. There were also buttons with little pictures on them, like an outline of the trunk, a picture of an open hood, or a wavy line, presumably indicating the cigarette lighter or heater. There was even a schematic drawing of the car, below which was written MESSAGE CENTER. There were no messages. Nowhere, either, was there anything that looked like a gas-cap release.

I told the children to fan out and to look for a button with something looking like a gas pump, possibly a picture of a drop, a nozzle, or even the word "gas." One of them finally found it. It was inside the glove compartment.

Just when I've mastered proper use of the SHIFT LOCK OVERRIDE button and other idiosyncrasies, the new models come out and I have to start all over again.

THE SHOW ON
THE ROAD

Like many New Yorkers, we have a place outside of the city. I hesitate to call it the country, because it is less so all the time, and now it's much easier to spot a condominium up there than it is a cow. Whatever it's called, we have two lives—really three. The third is that period between the other two when, on the weekend, the car brings us all together and keeps us that way for a few hours.

The worst part of the trip is always leaving Manhattan. Whatever route we take, the way is dotted with teenagers armed with squeegees (and big muscles). Assuming you're willing to pay for speck-free vision, they throw themselves on the windshield, often before the car has come to a stop. Never mind that their buddies down the block have just performed the same service. The charge is discretionary, but if you're perceived as too stingy, you can end up buying some new glass. Thus, no matter what way we go, we're sure to leave the island with a clean windshield.

By the time we're finally under way, it's usually quite late. Backseat chatter soon dies down, and all that's audible is the *bizzz, bizzz, bizzz* of the headphones that have put our children to sleep. This is when I debrief my wife about the events of the week. I learn about the kids' academic and social lives, the triumphs and the setbacks. I find out what new trade has been added to the payroll, and we usually run through the latest orthodontic developments before completing the trip.

We come back on Sunday afternoon. Preparations are frantic as we try to cram all we can into the day and still get back by dinnertime. If we're late, there's a heavy price to pay, as the kids get increasingly crabby as mealtime approaches. A graph of this phenomenon would show a line representing the amount of food in the stomach descending diagonally toward an ascending line of irritability. They intersect, explosively, at about 7:00 P.M.

Packing for the return is always a challenge. Each time I am asked to defy basic principles of volume and mass by getting a small mountain of bags and loose items from the driveway into the trunk. Instructions like "Don't put anything on top of my blowfish" and "Be sure to put my dollhouse furniture on top" (along with the shell collection, the ironed clothes, the papier mâché volcano science project, the flowers, and the eggs) don't make it any easier. The final stages of packing are done quickly and when no one is looking.

Once we're under way, the trip is much more animated than was the Friday night drive. Sometimes the kids will play a round or two of Pinch Bug. The object of this game is to get points by being the first to spot VW Beetles. Sightings are reported orally. The three of them quickly developed the same level of expertise such that whenever a Beetle comes barely into view, all three scream, *"PINCH BUG!!!"* in deafening unison. I don't think much of that game.

Silence during the trip would be unusual. Our conversations (using the term loosely) vary, but often sound like this:

DAUGHTER 1:	Carrie won't give me a Mamba.
DAUGHTER 2:	I bought these Mambas with my own money.
ME:	What's a Mamba?
DAUGHTER 1:	Yesterday I gave Carrie a Gummi Bear, and she still won't give me a Mamba.
DAUGHTER 2:	You only gave me a Gummi Bear because I let you use my Def Leppard tape. Besides, a Mamba is much bigger than a Gummi Bear.
ME:	What's a Mamba?
DAUGHTER 1:	You let me use your Def Leppard tape because I let you listen to White Snake. Besides, I gave you two Gummi Bears, and they're as big as a Mamba.
ME:	WHAT IN GOD'S NAME IS A MAMBA!!?
	(Silence)
WIFE:	You don't have to shout.
DAUGHTER 2:	Yeah, Dad. You tell *us* not to shout.
SON:	(Always quick to generalize when it's to his advantage) Okay. That means that now it's all right for us to shout.

I think a Mamba is something you eat.

Our children were quick to learn the rules of the road.

DAUGHTER 1:	Mom, I just saw a sign that said, "Speed limit fifty-five MPH." Why is Daddy going sixty?
SON:	Okay. That means that we don't have to obey rules either.

Sometimes, though, we actually get things done. This is a good time to practice parts for the school play. I find that

I end up memorizing the lines, too, to the point where, as I sat in my office one spring, some of Gepetto's words kept running through my head.

Our most ambitious project one year was helping our son with his spelling. Getting him ready for a test was like preparing a knight for battle. Nancy would test him by reading words from the sheet he'd written them on. That's not as easy as it sounds, because his school, I think, teaches handwriting by having the boys copy medical prescriptions at high speed. When it seemed that a word on his sheet reflected a spelling not widely accepted (a frequent tip-off was the presence of five consonants in a row) my wife and I would try to reach a consensus. If that couldn't be done, or when a reasonable doubt still remained, Carrie, a dictionary in her lap, was ready with a definitive resolution. And so, as the collective might of our family was loosed on words like "chrysanthemum" and "onomatopoeia," we headed south.

Back in Manhattan, after the windshield has been washed three or four times, we're home.

When our children were younger, they liked nothing better than to get out of the city each weekend so they could run around on the grass, listen to the birds, and play in the dirt. The older they get, however, the more resistant they are to going away. Why, they want to know, should they have to go to the country, where there are only four outdoor sports, a big garden, a soft lawn, and a tree house their father built for them, when they could be playing Nintendo in a friend's apartment?

We used to go away every Friday and have now negotiated a once every other weekend schedule. I don't like the direction of the trend.

OUR SIDES OF THE FAMILY

HOLIDAY preparations were never very important in my family. When Christmas approached, we'd go to the woods and pick out a tree. We weren't particularly fussy. If it had pine needles and fit through the door, it was fine. As we grew older, my parents saw no point in going through an entire tree each year and my father would hack off a branch and prop it up in a corner. They also had a minimalist's approach to wrapping gifts—with large or awkwardly shaped items, only the parts that showed from underneath the Christmas tree (or branch) were covered with paper. As a child, I had only to shift my viewing angle to find out if a particular box came from L. L. Bean or F.A.O. Schwarz. What was important to my parents was the day itself, and to them things like elaborate wrapping paper were distractions.

The same went for Thanksgiving. The first year we were married, Nancy and I went to have dinner with my parents,

as did my brothers, sister, and her family. The meal was standard, with a big juicy turkey and lots of stuffing. As we were having coffee afterward, my sister started to look a bit gray. Holding her stomach, she got up, eased herself out of the room, and went upstairs. Soon we could hear the plumbing at work. A few minutes later, my brother-in-law became pale, and he, too, excused himself. Within the next hour, almost all of us had been sick. The diagnosis was the flu, which was going around, and we remarked on the coincidence of it hitting so many of us at the same time.

A year later, the same group reconvened for another turkey dinner. This time everyone got sick. When we felt good enough to travel and were about to go, Nancy decided to ask my mother how she had prepared the turkey. My mother, as it turned out, was not about to spend the day in the kitchen when she could be talking with her children and grandchildren. She therefore had had everything ready a few days ahead of time. That's also when she stuffed the turkey. I gather that if you want to make a fertile breeding ground for particularly virulent bacteria, that's about the best way to do it. We still go to my parents for Thanksgiving, but now we have ham.

My wife reflects the influence of a very different kind of family. She will start baking Christmas cookies as soon as Thanksgiving is over, panicked because she's already received baked goods from her sister, who started on Columbus Day. The Christmas tree must touch the ceiling and have a height-to-width ratio of 1.5:1, not 2:1, like a lot of the trees you see. She sets aside a week to wrap the presents. That's in November.

On our first Christmas together, I was given a strong indication of how seriously my wife took holiday rituals. It was Christmas Eve, and we both worked that day, arriving home at about seven. Nancy put down her things, made up

a list, and said she was going out to get a goose. I was hungry and wanted to eat soon. Couldn't we have a steak? "*Steak?*" she asked. "Whoever heard of having a *steak* on Christmas Eve?" I told her I really didn't know what people ate on that day, but promised that if we had steak, I wouldn't tell anyone. It was out of the question. Off she went, returning an hour later with the goose and whatever you're supposed to eat with it. She took *The Joy of Cooking* down from the shelf, turned to "Poultry and Game Birds," and started to read. I picked up *The Decline and Fall of the Roman Empire* and turned to Chapter 1.

Hour after hour went by, and Nancy kept basting. We sat down to eat at 2:30 A.M. By then, it was no longer Christmas Eve, and we probably should have been eating something other than goose.

A DOG NEAR
THE MANGER

THERE's one thing I don't like about Christmas. Each year at this time, I'm made to feel bad when my children renew their request for a dog. I like animals, I really do. It's just that, together, we don't seem to have much luck.

We started with a goldfish. His (her?) first meal with us was breakfast. Mindful of our "You want it, you feed it" rule, my youngest daughter took it upon herself to give "Goldie" (Thomas wanted to name him "Jaws") his morning meal. She poured some fish food into his bowl, put about the same amount of Rice Krispies into hers, and sat down to eat. She had probably given him enough to keep fair-sized bluefish fully nourished for a week, so I scooped it out and sprinkled in a few flakes. The following morning, the fish was floating on his side, staring at our recessed lighting. Annie thought he was asleep. I explained that the average goldfish needs very little sleep, and rarely nods off in the position we were observing. She wasn't convinced, but finally let me throw him away. Her opinion of me, however, had not been improved by the episode. Either I had thrown away a perfectly good fish who was only napping, or had starved the thing to death.

A year later, my other daughter came home with two mice, graduates of her school's science department. By the end of their first week with us, the mice looked none too healthy. My son had the flu at the time, and Nancy thought it possible that he had passed it on to the mice. After making due allowance for the difference in body weight between a 120-pound boy and a 4-ounce mouse, she measured some of his streptomycin into their water supply. There was no improvement, and we all decided to accelerate their life cycles. One night I was handed a Kleenex box containing the mice and was told to dispose of them. The goldfish experience had established me as the only family member whose heart was sufficiently black to be able to do the dirty work.

Then we got Francis the cat. He developed a daily routine of counting the knots per square inch in the Oriental rug after autographing the piano. As Francis found new items to shred, I decided that his front claws did not serve a useful purpose. When he came home from the vet without them and minus his libido (included in the price), Francis, who had been overanesthetized, seemed barely alive. Each child squinted at me with an icy stare. For a while, they ate their meals in silence, without lifting their eyes from the table. Now and then, we discuss whether Francis should be let outside. My wife advises against it, because he can't defend himself. As if on cue, the kids snap their heads in my direction and say in unison, "Yeah [pause] Dad." In such moments, I point out that my conduct was comparatively blameless and refer to the friend who backed

his station wagon over the family cat. That never seems to help.

It got worse. One day my son came home with a hamster and cage he'd bought with his own money. A few mornings later, I was in the kitchen, where we kept the cage, tidying up. As I was putting out the garbage, I thought

I heard a rustling sound, but didn't give it much thought. When my son came in, he asked if I had seen the hamster. I learned that the previous evening he had shut the door to the kitchen and opened the cage so the hamster could roam about all night. The animal couldn't be located, and must have found his way into the garbage bag that I had thrown out. By a vote of three to one, the family decided not to observe Father's Day that year.

After the hamster incident, there wasn't any talk about a dog for a long time. It started again just before Christmas. I tell my children that we should go more slowly and first see how we make out with another goldfish.

OF MICE AND MODEMS

I come from a long line of holdouts. We, I am sure, were the last family on the East Coast to get a television. My parents deflected every appeal for one with lectures about homogenized brains and deteriorating eyesight, concluding with an exaltation of the printed word. To watch *The Cisco Kid* or *Superman,* my siblings and I had to befriend every contemporary on our street. So as not to overdo it with any one of them, we rotated their TV rooms like corn and alfalfa.

When our parents finally buckled under our united and relentless pressure, it was not done with grace. A used ten-inch black-and-white set was unceremoniously placed on the bare floor in an unheated, unfurnished bedroom, and a straight-backed kitchen chair was put in front of it. TV viewing was therefore either prone or downhill.

Decisions on clothing reflected the same philosophy. My father, for example, tried to avoid wearing suits from clothiers that were still in business. With influences such as these, I found my own behavior increasingly consistent with what should be the family motto: Hold Out. Hold On. I have great difficulty throwing anything away. What if I ever needed it?

When I got married to a seemingly normal girl from Chicago, I wondered what she would make of my genetic baggage. The signs were encouraging. I soon learned that things she was through with were not discarded but were boxed, labeled, and tucked away. A representative box was labeled BLUE GOWN/JUNIOR PROM 1956. I suspected that had I looked on the other side of the box, I would have found the name of her date.

Back in the days of our first apartment, when space was very precious, we started to compute its size not in square feet but in cubic inches. One day we were getting ready for dinner guests. These preparations were like a scavenger hunt. China, for example, did not have a place of its own, but went where it could be squeezed. At one point, I was closing in on some dishes in the closet when I found my way blocked by a large box I had never noticed before. I pulled it out and found the label. It read PIECES OF STRING TOO SHORT TO USE.

This is what our children are up against when they lobby us to make a purchase, particularly if it's something that plugs in. Most recently, the pitch was for a computer. The rationale had surface appeal. Whatever we thought of computers themselves, the word-processing function could be used by everyone in the family. I pointed out that we have a perfectly good electric typewriter, which got me through college and law school. My son says it's so old that when you hit *s,* the machine prints *f,* but that isn't true.

As the months went by, they wore us down. We decided that a computer would be that year's Christmas present from everyone to everyone. I set out to learn about the things, entering the world of the mouse and the modem. I learned that some computers are friendly to users and that some communicate with each other, though not necessarily the friendly ones. I learned that certain kinds of computers even have clones, but that's apparently okay. That's about all I learned. I listened to computer salesmen for hours, nodding, I think, at the right times. None of it sank in, but I finally made a choice. Several big white boxes showed up under the tree that year.

The machine is hooked up, and it's being used. On his last try, my son moved a little ball through a graphic maze in 124 seconds. That's a 17 percent improvement over his previous effort. Annie can write her name 150 times in the shape of a rabbit. No one has yet learned how to make it function as a word processor. That doesn't bother me as much as the headline that appeared on page 1 of *The New York Times* two days after that Christmas:

IBM ANNOUNCES BREAKTHROUGH
Existing Home Computers Will Be
Obsolete Within A Year, Spokesman Says

I was right all along. Hold Out. Hold On.

HIGHER (AND FARTHER) LEARNING

Our son's school ends in ninth grade. On the assumption that New York City is no place for a young man bursting with adolescent energy, we spent much of the fall during his last year visiting and applying to boarding schools. Given the amount of time we devoted to the effort, we are probably qualified to be consultants in the process.

First we had to decide which schools to visit. We selected about ten, based on reputation and the recommendation of the placement director at Thomas's school. The list, however, was not static. As the horror stories came in—"The [name of couple]'s son went to [name of school], had a B+ average, was captain of the crew, and couldn't get into *any* Ivy League college"—a school would be dropped off the list. It was restored when we learned what a stinker the kid was. After several drafts, we had our final list.

The Catalog

We then sent away for the school catalogs. These things are gorgeous. In terms of paper quality, photography, and layout, they are in the same league as IBM's annual report. As a means, however, of selecting one school over another, these booklets are not particularly helpful. Each will have pictures of:

1. Two or three smiling students of both sexes, usually with braces, carrying heavy books across a well-maintained courtyard;

2. A class being conducted on the lawn with the shirt-sleeved teacher resting one hand on a golden retriever;

3. An action shot of an athletic contest captioned with the final and winning score; and

4. A picture of the youthful headmaster, who projects firmness tempered by gentle understanding.

There is a certain sameness, too, to their texts, which tout "the [name of school] experience" and "the [name of school] community." Many of the adjectives ("broadening," "exciting," and "growing") overlap, as do the nouns ("responsibility," "commitment," and "challenge"). Based on these catalogs, one would jump at the chance to attend any of these places, so a visit to each one is needed.

The Visit

The best day for a visit is Saturday morning. On that day, our son wouldn't miss any classes, I wouldn't miss work, and as most schools have Saturday classes, one can get a good feel of each place. Saturday morning appointments, however, are harder to get than matinee tickets to *The Phantom of the Opera*. We, though, were able to get one for our first visit, and set out on a Friday evening to spend the night at a motel near the school.

The visit is not just for the applicant and his parents to look over the school. It was also when Thomas would have his interview, and so, as we drove along, we went over some questions he was likely to get. We discussed favorite subjects, teachers he liked, outside interests, career plans, and books he had recently read. We also had him try answers to some difficult questions, like how he would explain his one low grade in an otherwise very good record. We counseled against his proposed answer: "The teacher was a jerk," suggesting that he speak in terms of an inexplicable inability to get motivated. We thought he should have some questions of his own, and he came up with:

1. How early do classes start in the morning?
2. Is chapel mandatory?
3. Is there room inspection?
4. What are the visiting hours at the girls' dorms?

We told him that a better list might be:

1. Could he take Russian *and* two other languages?
2. Can one be excused from Saturday night social activities to do community service?
3. What is the origin of the school emblem, whose Latin motto he had translated?

At the school the following day, we got a short lesson in something that hadn't even occurred to us—suitable attire.

Waiting in the lounge ahead of us was another family. The father wore a navy suit and a white-collared pink shirt monogrammed on the cuff. His fourteen-year-old son had on black wing-tipped loafers with red-and-blue Argyle socks. Mom was swathed in an ankle-length mink. I thought to myself that if they accept this kid, they'll put the family down for a new science building. The very pleasant looking admissions director appeared in her wool cardigan and greeted them. She eyed the fur coat with a look that said, "If I put aside an entire year's salary, I probably could afford one of those sleeves."

After greeting us, she said that a student would be taking us on a tour that included the library, classrooms, athletic facilities, and the dining room. When we asked if it would be possible to see a dormitory room, she said that we certainly could, but she thought it would be a waste of time. There was so much more to see, and a dormitory room is a dormitory room—walls, door, and possibly a window. We repeated the request, and she told our young guide, who by then had joined us, to add a room to the tour.

We set out and were shown facilities that could only be described as fabulous. There were bright classrooms with floor-to-ceiling windows looking out on the autumn colors, and a quiet lake, gleaming science labs, and athletic facilities that would have been more than adequate for any Big Ten school. We also saw a dorm room. It was difficult to tell how high the ceilings were, because we couldn't locate the floor. Entering the room was out of the question, and from the doorway, we looked in on an area where we were able to identify a computer, stereo, guitar, and lacrosse stick, all poking out from under a layer of clothing and bedding. It looked like a landslide, with the higher portion probably coinciding with the location of the bed or beds (we couldn't tell if it was a single, double, or triple). The walls were decorated with posters of rock stars and girls in bikinis.

After the tour, we had the interview. The admissions director spoke first to our son, then to us. We told her how wonderful the school was. She agreed. She told us how wonderful our son was. We agreed. Driving home, we debriefed Thomas on his interview. Our preparation of the evening before had, of course, been useless. She, for example, had asked him if he had to be a fruit, what kind would he be and why? She had also asked him who he would most like to be if he could be anyone at all. What a great opportunity, I thought. As my wife asked how he had answered, I quickly wondered whether he would pick someone like Winston Churchill or Albert Schweitzer. Then I thought he'd probably pick his father. That's it, it would be me. He, instead, had named a friend of ours who doesn't work and has devoted his life to trying to make the U.S. Olympic luge team. As the seasons change, he follows the snow back and forth across the Equator. Thomas told the admissions director that he'd made this choice because this guy seems to be having fun all the time. Great. She had also asked him if he went into space, what three things would he take? Here it comes, I thought. He'll say a television, a VCR, and a CD player. As he told us his answer —some seeds, the biggest book he could find, and his cat—I settled back in my seat.

Over the next six weeks, we visited about ten different schools. At a few of them, the condition of the buildings was such that you knew a capital drive would be announced shortly after you signed up for the place. Most, however, had wonderful facilities. The student bodies themselves had very different looks. Even at schools where jackets and ties were required, there was a variety. At some, the students were right out of the Orvis catalog; at others the look was more early Prohibition—black shirts and pink ties. Where jackets weren't required, the outfit was baggy pants with holes, T-shirts, and baseball caps worn backward. No matter what the school, however, every boy and girl wore boat shoes.

The Application

The next step is the application. This isn't simply a matter of filling in a few blanks and sending off a transcript with a teacher recommendation. The application is work. The first page asks about the applicant's family situation. In the old days, a description would have been put on one line. The computer age has expanded the space required for that information to an entire page of boxes. You must check whether the applicant's parents are:

1. married and living together;
2. married and living apart;
3. unmarried and living together;
4. unmarried and living apart.

As for the living arrangement, you have to check whether the applicant is living with:

1. both parents;
2. mother;
3. father;
4. mother and stepfather;
5. father and stepmother;
6. mother and friend, with a box to check (optional) if the mother and friend are of the same sex;

7. father and friend (with the same box);
8. other.

There is then an array of additional optional boxes, asking for information on race, religion, and disabilities.

The application also asks for an essay, in the applicant's own handwriting (a directive they would regret in my son's case). A representative topic was:

> Describe the most significant experience in your life to date and explain how it has changed you. Give particular emphasis to the kind of person you were both before the incident and afterwards, focusing also on new goals which you set for yourself as a result of the experience and the schedule you have established for achieving them.

The applicant is frequently asked to complete a series of sentences like "People who know me think that I am . . ." "The quality I admire most in other people is . . ." and "My biggest weakness is . . ." My wife and I considered giving him suggestions, but realized that would be unnecessary when we saw him write, "My biggest weakness is that I am too much of a perfectionist."

One evening, our oldest daughter quietly borrowed one of the applications. She returned it the next morning, having finished the sentences for him with suggestions such as:

The hardest decision I ever had to make was . . .
whether to watch *Three's Company* or *Family Ties.* They were both on at the same time.

I feel good about myself when . . .
I resist the temptation to pull my sister's hair.

Other than my parents, one person I admire greatly is . . .
my sister. She is beautiful, brilliant, and very talented.

No two applications were the same or even similar, and an essay prepared for one school was never usable for another. Somehow, though, they all got done.

After countless hours on the Massachusetts Turnpike, tour after tour, and essay upon essay, Thomas decided to continue his schooling in New York City.

THE FEMALE OF THE SPECIES

WHEN our son bounded into adolescence, I thought I should have a talk with him about the female of the species. I had previously covered mechanical matters, and he had obviously picked up a good deal of information on his own. Years before then, he showed me that he had acquired an early mastery of the subject.

I had taken up running and would go out in the evening. One of my first outings was on a hot, heavy spring night. I returned, a wet, exhausted mess and collapsed in the living room, where Thomas was doing his homework. He was eleven at the time. As my recovery slowly progressed, he looked over at what was obviously not a happy man and asked, "Why do you do this, Dad?" I explained that I thought it was time I exerted a bit of control over my body and shed a few pounds. Still looking at me, he cocked his head and asked, "New secretary?"

Knowing that his foundation was solid, my purpose this

time was to prepare him for his contacts with girls, which would inevitably increase, by making him aware of some more subtle, but very important differences between men and women.

The kind of difference I had in mind was similar to one that exists between him and his oldest sister. His room always looks as though it has just been subjected to a Gestapo search. Hers would sail through a West Point inspection. The same difference was at work in the way they went about preparing for the first time they went away. My daughter's first trip was to Florida, where she had been invited to visit a classmate over spring vacation. Two weeks before the trip, she prepared a list of things to pack. The list had general categories, such as "clothing," broken down into subcategories of "footwear," "dressy clothes," "T-shirts," and so on. Within each subcategory, individual items, with quantity, were identified. Next to each item she had drawn two boxes. The first was to indicate a preliminary decision to take an item along. A check in the second box meant that the item had been packed. This, I learned, was the first draft of her list.

Carrie was completely packed three days before she left. She also had a duplicate list, to be used when she packed to come home. When she got back, she reported that she hadn't forgotten anything. She also had been able to supply those who had, letting them use her dental floss, extra radio batteries, and the spare shoelaces she'd brought along.

When Thomas went away, it was to camp, and at 6:00 P.M. on the day before he left, he had not started packing. That night he put his duffel bag in the middle of his room and threw things into it. He looked like Magic Johnson practicing shooting hoops from different parts of the floor. After dropping him off at camp, my wife and I predicted that we'd get a series of collect calls asking us to Federal Express his swimming suit, sunglasses, and other overlooked items to him. Those calls never came. We don't know if, like his sister, he remembered everything, or if he viewed things he forgot as nonessential, and went without a toothbrush or underwear for five weeks. Although it would probably be risky to generalize too much, I believe that gender was at work here.

Moving to areas from my personal experience with adults,

I told him that he should not expect women to be mechanically adept. Take his mother, for example. She has had a camera—the same one—for twenty years, but is incapable of changing the film. Whenever a roll is finished, she will hand me the camera, her arm fully extended, with the camera sitting on an arched palm much the way we were taught to give an apple to a horse. The gesture is accompanied by a sour look and a helpless whimper.

The same applies to our music equipment. Nancy hardly ever turns it on, but there's one tape she likes to listen to at Christmastime. Year after year, she will ask me to play the tape. Each time I give her a five-second course on how to do it herself. It's not particularly complicated. There are two pieces of equipment. On one she has to push "power" and "tape" and on the other "power" and "play." She refuses to master this information, saying, "Four buttons? I have to push four buttons just to play one tape?" I explain that they don't have to be pushed in any particular sequence, like a push-button combination lock, nor is speed a factor, as it is on those devices that prevent you from starting a car if you're drunk. It's wasted breath.

The most important difference, however, is women's memories. They are awesome. The time will come, I told my son, when he will start seeing a girl regularly. She will remember the date and time they met and the place. She will remember what kind of a day it was, down to its temperature/humidity index and the composer and artist of any music within earshot. She will remember what he was wearing, what she had on, and what they talked about. She will remind him of these details at each anniversary (at first celebrated monthly) of this encounter, punctuating her account with an occasional "Don't you remember anything?"

If he gets married, he will develop an even greater appreciation of the female memory. Conversations such as the following will be regular occurrences:

WIFE: We've been asked to dinner by George and Susan Edgar.

ME: Edgar?

WIFE: Yes. You remember, they were at that party Bob and Dale gave two years ago just before Christmas. Remember, we talked with that psychiatrist from San Diego whose wife wore those funny glasses with green rims?

ME: Green rims?

WIFE: That's right, and we talked with that short, bald lawyer from Boston whose wife worked at the Aquarium. They had a girl at Milton and two boys at Exeter. He was the one who collected duck decoys.

ME: Duck decoys?

WIFE: Yes, and Dale served those wonderful hors d'oeuvres. Remember, the little square ones covered with sun-dried tomatoes?

ME: Sun-dried tomatoes?

And so on. I told my son that he shouldn't be impressed by such recall or disturbed by his inability to remember his wedding anniversary, the wedding anniversaries of parents and in-laws, birthdays of children, or birthdays of godchildren. Men are good at other things. I would go into that at another time.

THE RIGHT FORK

Lᴵᴷᴱ most parents, my wife and I have an ongoing effort to teach our children the social graces—at least the ones we ourselves have been able to pick up. Much time, for example, has been spent on the thank-you note. After Christmas or a birthday, the child is badgered until the last gift has been acknowledged. Counseling on the content of the message is often involved, particularly when the reaction to the present is something like "But I hate the stupid thing." In those moments, we try to guide our children along the narrow path between hypocrisy and candor.

They, in turn, use such occasions to observe that, as families go, we are unique. The conversation always begins with either "Nobody else" or "Everyone else." "Nobody else," we learn, has to write a thank-you note for every single present, goes to bed when they do, and so on. We also learn that "everyone else" gets a bigger allowance than they do, is allowed to see movies we won't let them watch, etc. Our response—"If everyone else [description of something foolish], would you?"—only makes them groan and roll their eyes toward the ceiling.

Much of our instruction is intended to prepare them for when they are guests in other people's homes. There is, however, only so much you can teach. No matter what we do, our children will never be adequately prepared for the situations that regularly arise when one's eating at someone else's table.

As an initial matter, if you're invited to dinner, when should you arrive? If you show up at or close to the time on the invitation, you will be the first one there. The other guests will trickle in, and there will be cocktails for a couple of hours. You will fill up on hors d'oeuvres, and have little interest in the meal when it's finally served. If you plan on appearing midway through a long cocktail hour, you will arrive to find everyone standing behind chairs at the table, waiting for you.

I used to think that, either way, you were safe arriving half an hour late, but you're not. One summer we were invited to a 6:00 P.M. family picnic. We arrived at six-thirty and sat down to have a drink while the children played on the lawn. As I helped myself to a handful of nuts from a bowl, I noticed the grill, which looked very cold, beside which was the charcoal, still in the bag.

At 8:00 P.M., there had been no visible progress in getting the meal under way. The host and hostess were chatting away, and the grill was still cold. The nuts were all gone. I calculated that if the coals were lighted that very minute, something not too thick could be ready to eat by eight forty-five. At eight-thirty, the kids no longer had the strength to play, and were sitting at our feet. Our hostess was stretched out on a deck chair. Looking up at the cigarette smoke she had just exhaled, she called to the kitchen, where her husband was making another round of drinks, "Honey, did you remember to pick up some chicken?" Our children looked up at us with all the anguish their weak bodies could muster.

Something else you have to decide is whether to bring something like flowers or a bottle of wine to your hostess. If you do, she will make a big fuss over your gift and your thoughtfulness in front of the other guests, all of whom, it will be apparent, arrived empty-handed. When you are then introduced to these people, each of them will give you a tight smile. If you decide not to bring something, you will be alone. One by one, the other guests will arrive, handing over bouquets of roses and bottles of fine wine. As your hostess greets each one with something like, "Oh, Peter, what lovely flowers! Dear, look at the flowers Peter brought," you will examine artwork on the walls or inspect the tops of your shoes.

Once you're seated, different questions are presented. For example, you're at a dinner party, the first course (soup) has just been cleared, and a small mound of pasta is put in front of you. Is this some kind of appetizer or the main course? You're famished, and the soup didn't make a dent in your hunger. You look for clues. After this course, there will still be a knife and a fork left. They look as though they might be for salad, which wouldn't fill you up any more than the soup did, but you're not familiar with this pattern. The host and hostess don't look like big eaters, and that little bit of food is probably enough to keep them going. You are not simply curious; you want to know what to do if they come around again with the pasta.

You will guess wrong. If you conclude that the remaining knife and fork are for a hearty meat course and decline seconds, you will be served an endive with a slice of tomato. As you finish the salad and the dessert of a scoop of sorbet and you despair of the after-dinner conversation ever ending, all you can think about is going home and making a sandwich.

On the other hand, if you load up on pasta when it's passed, that course is sure to be followed by a platter of garnished veal chops.

Then there's the question of the bread-and-butter plate. My wife tells me it's always on your left, and this I've memorized. Not everybody has. You will be sitting at a dinner and see the person to your left, talking with the one on her left, reach to her right and grab your roll. You look across the table and see your hostess taking butter from the plate she's supposed to use. The guests are now foreclosed from compensating for the error by having everyone shift to the right. Someone's going to get burned, and you decide it's not going to be you. After all, you were the one who first spotted the problem, and besides, you want a roll. You slide your hand along the tablecloth and circle your fingers around the roll to your right. Just then your dinner partner to the right interrupts her conversation to shoot a cold stare at you, and then at your hand, which she has caught resting on her plate. You give her a sheepish grin, nodding quickly in the direction of the person who started the whole thing, but she turns away.

Mastering the proper use of eating utensils is no less difficult. Here again, I memorized the basic rule: Start from the outside and move in. In the case of a crowded table, there is a possibility that, if you start from too far to the outside, you will invade someone else's place setting, but that risk is small. The difficulty usually comes when you've completed a course, having found it unnecessary to use the knife that appears to have been intended for that course. You will do the wrong thing with it. If you decide you should have used the knife instead of the edge of your fork

to cut whatever it was and put it on your plate, the waiter will remove it, placing it back on the table. Having spent some time with what's left on your plate, the knife will make a greasy spot on the tablecloth. If you leave the knife where it was, the waiter will take it away. In both instances, the waiter will pick up the knife the same way he would handle a dead bug.

There are two ways of avoiding these kinds of embarrassments. Follow someone else's lead. Most people, however, don't know any more than you do, so that isn't the solution. Many seem to prefer the second way. Stay home.

HAPPY BIRTHDAY

MY wife and I have given a total of forty-two birthday parties for our children. For reasons I'll explain, that is more than one per year per child. Although each one was different, there was a pattern.

In New York, many parents have visions of chocolate cake being ground into the chintz, or a game of Pin the Tail on the Donkey getting out of hand amid their spindly-legged antiques. The birthday invitation therefore will often be to neutral spots ranging from a McDonald's, where a section of the room has been roped off, to the *QE2,* which has been chartered for the afternoon. All of our children's birthday celebrations were at home, and the evidence is still visible.

With us, celebration of the first birthday can't really be called a party. Our son was seated at the head of the dining-room table, surrounded on three sides by a battery of grandparents, parents, uncles, and a couple of neighbors.

Each one had a camera. As the cake was lowered in front of him, each camera was raised to the eye in anticipation of him doing something worth recording. He obliged. Suddenly, and without warning, he took an overhand swipe, much like a tennis serve, and imbedded his open palm in the top of the cake. Flash attachments blazed. He then put his frosting-covered hand in his mouth, having, along the way, left the excess on the tablecloth, chair seat, and new birthday outfit. With presents, but without cleanup, the whole thing didn't last more than fifteen minutes.

The format for the second birthday was the same. The crowd, though, had thinned (no grandparents or uncles), and the chairs had been Scotchguarded.

By our son's third birthday, we decided to invite some of his contemporaries. Sitting at a table between members of the opposite sex whom he had never met, would probably never see again, and probably wouldn't care for would be good practice for the adult dinner party. We therefore asked some friends with children the same age as Thomas to come with them to his party. It was probably the first social function for each of these children. They ignored the games we'd organized and hid behind their mother's legs, which they grabbed like tree trunks. When they were made to sit down, the guests spent most of the time sobbing and twisting themselves in their chairs as they raised their arms to their parents standing behind. Thomas couldn't understand why they were crying. He was having a great time.

By the time of his fourth birthday, our son was in school. Shortly after he was accepted, we got three pieces of mail from the school: a tuition bill, a solicitation from the "Development Office," and a Notice re Birthday Parties. The notice informed us of an important school policy. To prevent hurt feelings, if a child asks someone in the class to a birthday, everyone in the class should be invited. This meant we could now count on a guest list of fifteen for our son's birthday celebrations. His class was divided in half, and if he befriended someone in the other section, the number grew to thirty.

As Thomas was moving through this progression, his sisters were too. A representative party for them was Carrie's fourth. That was a two-section party. With a group that size, the trick is to find something to keep them amused for the hour and a half when they're not eating birthday cake. The previous week, a classmate's party had been at Tavern on the Green, which had been taken over for the occasion. They had two magicians and three clowns from the Ringling Brothers/Barnum & Bailey Circus. After the cake, the children all had pony rides in Central Park. That seemed to work out well.

We rented a VCR and *Dumbo*. We quickly learned that, except for Carrie and one other girl, everyone in the class had seen *Dumbo*. They had also seen every Disney film you could name, all the James Bond movies, and most of the *Rocky* series. As Carrie and the other deprived child watched *Dumbo*, twenty-eight children explored our apartment. Those kids, I'm afraid, couldn't wait to get home and turn on *Friday the 13th* or something else more their speed.

Somewhere along the line, we started celebrating each child's birthday twice. This is because Thomas was born in July, when his school friends are away. We therefore started celebrating his birthday during the school year. When his real birthday came around, it, of course, couldn't be ignored, so we would have a second, albeit modest, celebration on that day as well. His sisters then allowed as how they, too, would like to double the number of their birthdays. Very soon, we were doing six a year. When this started to interfere with our observance of the major holidays, we discontinued the practice.

One year we decided to do something different for a birthday. When Carrie, who plays the piano, turned seven, we asked if she would like to go to a concert at Carnegie Hall. She said she would, and I got us tickets to hear Rudolf Serkin.

The evening came, and it was going to be perfect. Carrie, in a red velvet dress Nancy had worn when she had been that age, and I went off together and had dinner before the concert. After dinner we found our seats, in the front row of a box with an ideal view of the stage. The concert was on the occasion of Serkin's eightieth birthday, and the place was packed.

When the music started, the hall quieted instantly. As I listened, drinking in the music, the evening, and the look on my daughter's face, I became aware of a loud ticking sound in back of us. I turned around, and my attention was instantly drawn to the watch on the wrist of a man seated behind Carrie. It was huge, and looked as though it were capable of receiving satellite transmissions. How discourteous, I thought. I glared at the watch and turned around, assuming its owner would put the watch away or find some way of muffling the sound. The ticking continued. I couldn't believe anyone could be that insensitive and turned around again, giving the man and his watch an extra-fierce glare. There was no change. Now, I was getting mad, so mad that I couldn't hear the music anymore. This guy was ruining my evening. Obviously, I had been too subtle and would have to say something. I turned around again, and as I was opening my mouth, the offender leaned forward and whispered loudly, "It's not my watch. It's my heart."

We went back to celebrating birthdays at home.

SANTA'S LAST VISIT

SANTA Claus will probably visit our house for the last time this year. Our two oldest children turned from believers into co-conspirators long ago, but the youngest has held on, resisting playmates' attempts to convert her. She has not found it easy.

The most serious challenge to her conviction came when we went to see the Macy's Santa. I explained that we would be seeing someone who, while a surrogate Santa, had the ear of the man himself. For purposes of what would happen on Christmas, she could make believe he was the real thing.

On our way, we passed a number of Salvation Army volunteers dressed in their red-and-white outfits. We chatted with a particularly outgoing one, and I gave Annie some money to put in his pot. These people, I told her, were different from the make-believe Santa we were about to see. They, by way of contrast, were more in the nature of imitation Santas.

As we were about to enter Macy's, still another kind of Santa Claus approached us. He had on the red-and-white gear, but wore a black belt instead of the white ones we had seen on the Salvation Army people. A fur-trimmed cap looked odd on his shaved head. As we tried to walk by, he jammed a lollipop into my daughter's hand and shook a container for money in front of me. I bared my teeth, snarled, and as my daughter looked up at me with wide, uncomprehending eyes, we entered the store. To explain my conduct, I told her that unlike the make-believe Santa we were lining up for or the imitation Santa she had given money to, the one we had just brushed past was a fake Santa. Her expression didn't change.

The Santa Claus years have not been easy on the parents either. In our family, Santa comes on Christmas Eve while we're at church. That's a good trick. As we leave our apartment for the service, I will forget my overcoat or scarf, sending the rest of the family on ahead. Twenty minutes later, I join them in church and sit down quietly, trying to slow my breathing. I sit back, hoping my children won't notice the tributaries of sweat that run down my cheeks and merge under my chin, on an evening with the wind-chill factor usually keeping the temperature in the teens. I never wear a blue shirt on Christmas Eve.

The night before, my wife and I rarely get much sleep. In getting ready for Christmas Eve, the last thing we do is fill the stockings. That wouldn't be so difficult if Nancy didn't insist on removing the prices from every item—down to the last roll of lifesavers and chocolate bar. Everyone (even the cat) gets a stocking, and as I carefully peel off the prices, trying not to tear the wrapping, one radio announcer after another signs off for the night. One year I asked if bar coding was exempt, and got a negative ruling. From time to time, I question the necessity of the whole exercise, and my wife will impatiently tell me, "Santa doesn't shop at the five-and-dime." When I pursue it and ask why these things, which were obviously made by a conglomerate, could not have been picked up at a chain, she answers, "Keep peeling."

I didn't think my daughter could hold on for another year, but now I'm not sure what's going to happen. On Christmas night, as Annie was being tucked in, she confided in my wife, "I know there's no Santa Claus. But I still believe in him."

Part II

OUTDOORS

ALMOST SKIING

My wife and I introduced our children to skiing one winter. Mercifully, the season came to an end.

The first time we went, it took us three hours to get out of the house. For most of that time, the action upstairs looked like early Fellini—small people clad in underwear-white moving at half speed, all saying "Mom" over and over. "Mom" was not being sought for a specific problem of immediate concern. Instead, the expectation was that she, like TWA, would answer in the order in which she had been called. When the time came, they'd be ready with a request. Ready they were, with the likes of "I can't find my other sock" from a daughter as she headed off to play with the cat, trailing a sock, or "My parka isn't in there" from my son, waving in the direction of a closet without lifting his eyes from the book in his lap.

The sun was high in the sky by the time we had collected everything we'd need. Nancy had a bag of medical supplies, and was equipped to administer just about any noninvasive treatment. We also had isolated the requisite number of socks (two pair per child), underwear (both long and short), turtlenecks, sweaters, ski pants, parkas, mittens, hats, scarves, and other thermal items. Locating the clothing was only phase one. Getting it on each child's body involved some heavy negotiations over issues such as what a daughter was to do, with her favorite shirt in the wash, and whether my son should have to wear a sweater. He had stuck his hand out the window and insisted he didn't need one.

When we were finally ready to go, we were all so hungry that we sat down for a meal. Compressing our heavily insulated children, each one with an armload of audio equipment, into the backseat, we set off. At the three-mile mark, my son realized that he'd forgotten his sleek new sunglasses and didn't know how he could be expected to be seen in public without them. At the five-mile mark, the opposition to going back for the glasses had been defeated. We turned around, picked them up, and were finally on our way.

Once at the ski area, I set off to buy lift tickets. When given a quote for our family of five, I told the man with the tickets that he must have misunderstood me. We weren't interested in taking title to the mountain; we only wanted to slide down it a few times. There was no mistake. Rejoining the rest of the family, I found that my usually agile children had become virtually helpless. They were unable to buckle their boots, zip their parkas, or put on their mittens. In their defense, my wife had dressed them as if they were being suited up for the Nome-to-Fairbanks run, and they were teetering around like multicolored penguins.

After everything had been zipped, buttoned, snapped, or Velcroed shut, we tackled the equipment. It all worked except for one of my youngest daughter's bindings, which kept rejecting her boot. After I smashed the ski against a tree, the binding worked fine. I felt better too.

Most of what was left of the afternoon was spent in line. We were in line either for the lift, hot chocolate, or the bathroom. A trip to the bathroom was a team effort. A parent would hold the layers that had been peeled, like leaves from an artichoke, while the child shuffled along in line.

We also skied a bit that day, but I don't remember that part very well.

TENTING TONIGHT

ONE of my college literature courses focused for a semester on the theme of image versus reality. We studied Plato's "Cave" and although I don't remember the point, it was made by comparing shadows with what cast them. I find that the same theme runs through family activities. All too often, reality bears no relation to the image we turn over and carry around in our heads.

For us, camping is a good example. One summer our children talked us into spending a few days in the outdoors. As the day approached, my resistance broke down, and I began to warm to the idea. I would close my eyes and picture our happy little group at a campsite beside a clear mountain lake, cooking over an open fire as we whistled "We're Tenting Tonight." The reality was to be somewhat different.

As we were planning the trip, someone in the office observed that man has spent thousands of years getting up from the ground, out of caves, and down from the trees. She wondered why we wanted to reverse the process. I verbalized my image of the campsite by a mountain lake, inhaling deeply through my nose.

The day came, and after displacing most of the air in the car with supplies and borrowed gear, we were off. At the camping area, we found our site, unpacked, and set up the tents. I realized we were on a slope, but nothing could be done about that. We could decide later whether to sleep so that the blood rushed to our feet or to our heads.

After we were organized, we went down to the lake for a swim. On the way, we passed a line of parked motorcycles. Not a good sign. Back at our camp, we started a fire and cooked a good dinner. Image and reality were starting to merge. They quickly separated when we returned to the lake to wash the dishes. The tattooed owners of the motorcycles had appeared, producing their radios and beer. Eyeing them warily, we did the dishes, took a wide detour back, and went to bed.

My son and I shared a tent. I decided to put my head uphill; his went downhill. Nancy and the two girls in the other tent made a different decision. They slept sidehill. That apparently worked out fine except during those rare moments when they went to sleep. When they relaxed their grip on the hillside, they all rolled downhill, ending up like pieces of tumbleweed blown against a fence. My wife, at the bottom of the pile, would push her sleepy daughters back up the hill, and the cycle soon repeated itself. As I tried to get comfortable in one of the hot down-filled sleeping bags we'd borrowed, the motorcycle bunch started to warm up. Sleep was impossible. The music went on for a couple of hours, but suddenly stopped when they revved up and rode away. It had started to rain.

I found a flashlight and went out to cover up things that

shouldn't get wet, bringing back into the tent items that absolutely had to stay dry. Trying to wipe off my muddy feet, I settled carefully onto my sleeping bag. I had been told that a tent will leak if you touch it when it rains. I lay there very still, arms folded on my chest like a mummy. Several times during the night, I heard my daughters announce that they had to go to the bathroom. There was, of course, no such "room," and through the tent, I could see stabs of light as Nancy, first with one daughter and then the other, headed off into the wet woods with a flashlight. I was also able to hear her observations as the golf umbrella she carried repeatedly snagged on branches. Thomas slept soundly, with a trace of a smile on his face.

The rain stopped at some point during the night, and the August sun started working on our tents at about 5:00 A.M. My son was up at five-thirty, and I gave up trying to sleep an hour later. Outside, Thomas had built a fire, and was looking into it with that same smile on his face. It's all worth it, I said to myself. I said it over and over. The girls were scurrying around the campsite, tidying up and hanging wet things on tree branches. Their mother was still in her tent.

It has been said that my wife is not a morning person. That is certainly true, but it gets you only part of the way there. She doesn't think much of the early afternoon either. We could see the sides of the tent bulge out from time to time as she struggled to get comfortable, and could hear her exhale noisily as the frustration grew. At about 8:00 A.M., she emerged, slack-jawed, red-eyed, and expressionless. She made breakfast mechanically. After breakfast, the kids buzzed about, chattering away as they found different kinds of berries, discovered bird nests, and saw where some deer had slept. Nancy sat on a rock and stared at the ground.

We spent most of the day trying to keep our wet clothes in the sunny spots that moved around the campsite. After dinner, my wife, who did not talk much that day, and daughters went straight to bed. My son sat looking into the fire for over an hour.

It didn't rain that night. Instead, the woods were seemingly alive with all kinds of creatures. As Thomas slept, I could hear from the next tent, "What's that noise, Mommy?," "Did you hear that, Mommy?," and "I'm sure it's a bear, Mommy." Nancy kept reassuring the girls that the sounds were probably made by birds and chipmunks. A few times, however, her words weren't enough, and she was sent outside with a flashlight just to make sure.

The next morning, the children and I were up at six. At

seven, my wife pushed back the flap of her tent and, lifting her chin off of the ground, announced that she had had enough. We convened a quick family meeting and decided to cut the trip short. We cleaned up, packed, and drove home. During the drive, Nancy stared straight ahead. Her mouth was open, and she didn't appear to blink. After I had parked in our driveway, she eased herself onto the pavement. Leaving the car door open, she put one foot in front of the other and slowly walked into the house. She went straight to bed.

The following day, we unpacked, cleaned up, and sorted through the gear. Two of the sleeping bags we had borrowed were still wet and muddy. Nancy decided to wash them. At some point during the "spin" cycle, our washing machine began to sound unhealthy, and we noticed a burning smell. The down-filled sleeping bags, when wet, proved to be too much for the machine, and we had to have its motor replaced. When the sleeping bags themselves dried, all of the down stayed in a lump at one end. They were now useless, so we bought new bags to replace them.

After adding up our expenses for those two days in the woods, we calculated that it would have been far cheaper to have checked the whole family into the Plaza, where image and reality probably wouldn't have been quite so far apart.

ON FISHING

It seems that, at one time or another, fishing is a passion for every child. It certainly was for me. I spent hours casting and reeling in an empty lure, or watching my float sit quietly on the surface as everything in the lake ignored the juicy worm wiggling in the water below.

I remember two specific experiences about my fishing youth. In the first, a friend and I were fishing from a rowboat. I was reeling in my line when I heard my friend, who was in the bow, say, "Duck." At the same moment, my head was yanked forward. He had made an arching cast, and my ear had stopped the lure as it was picking up speed. Two terrified twelve-year-olds raced to shore and bicycled to the hospital in our town. I remember not appreciating the smiles on the doctors and nurses as I walked in with my rod and a large, multicolored lure swinging from my left earlobe. A young intern today would probably check to make sure I wanted it removed.

The second experience I remember was during the summer when we rented a house at the shore. Our first day there, I went to a nearby dock with my fishing rod and dropped a line in the water. I caught an eight-inch fish almost immediately. Within ten minutes, I had caught a dozen more. Swarms of fish hung around the dock pilings, and I probably didn't need to use bait. When I went home for lunch, I could barely carry the morning's catch, which I presented to my mother. I returned to the dock after lunch, and had similar success. Thus it went, day after day, for most of our two weeks there. I never knew what happened to the fish, because they certainly never appeared on the dinner table. The garden, however, seemed to grow very quickly during our short stay.

Our two oldest children retired from fishing very early, but Annie's enthusiasm for the sport only grows. The first time we went, I told her to dig for some worms while I pulled the gear together. The patience she was to show while fishing was not evident in her search for worms. When I was ready to go, I discovered that she had abandoned spot after spot, having given up on each one after a wormless spadeful, and the yard looked as though it had been the site of a frantic treasure hunt.

At the lake, it wasn't long before we had a strike. The rod barely bent as Annie reeled in a fish that would have looked more at home in a goldfish bowl than in the lake. She wanted to have it for dinner, but I explained that with the possible exception of tools for eye surgery, man has not developed an edge capable of scaling and fileting the fish she had caught.

Later we caught something more respectably sized, and took it home. Annie put it in a pail and watched it dart around. As dinner approached, she became ambivalent about eating her new friend, but curiosity was stronger than her affection, and I was asked to cook the fish. I put it on the kitchen counter, and as my daughter watched, I got out a knife and went to work. Annie's shoulders started to shake, and big tears rolled down her cheeks. When I asked what the matter was, she said, "I'm not used to seeing animals get their heads chopped off."

Annie rebounded from that experience, and her interest in the sport grew steadily, mainly from talking to a neighbor. This fellow is one serious fly-fisherman. Trout or fly motifs adorn his clothing accessories, and the fishing theme unifies his apartment. Picking out a Christmas present for him is never a problem. He's in his eighties, and as he has become less active, he has been giving Annie some of his fishing equipment. One day a fly rod, with a reel, line, and a box of flies, arrived. The rod itself is a thing of beauty— shiny bamboo, made, obviously by hand, in England, and signed by its maker. I know nothing about fly rods, but it was apparent even to me that this piece of equipment was special.

I hadn't a clue how one goes about this sport, and went to the library to read up on it. The first twelve chapters of the book I took out named, described, and showed pictures of different kinds of flies. I had always thought a fly was a fly, with possible categories for "the horsefly" and "the black fly," subdivided into "big" and "little." I was very wrong. I read, for example, about the Slate-gray Dun (*Heptagenia elegantula*), the Pale Morning Dun (*Ephemerella infrequens*), the Green Drake, Coffin Fly (*Ephemera guttulata*), the Light Cahill (*Stenomena interpunctatum*), and on and on. There were detailed drawings of the flies' heads, wings, and torsos. There was also some instruction, such as "How to tie an extended-body wiggle nymph" and "How to prepare a shaped wing from the webby part of a rooster hackle." My questions, however, were far more basic. I, for example, wanted to know how to attach the reel to the rod.

I got the equipment assembled and read up on casting (different book). Annie practiced on the lawn, and soon developed a long, smooth cast. Every few weeks, I'll take the rod out of the safe-deposit box and Annie and I will go fishing. She says she much prefers fly-fishing to fishing with worms. I think that's because we never catch anything.

Part III
In the Store

GET THE BIG EGGS, NOT THE LARGE ONES

FROM time to time and usually as my wife is preparing dinner, I'm asked to pick up a last-minute item at the grocery store. I hate doing this, not because of the effort involved, but because of the decisions I'm called upon to make.

A good example is the hurried request my wife made one evening for a dozen eggs. It would be hard to get that one wrong, but just to make sure, I asked if she wanted any particular size. "Large" came the response.

Off I went and, sure enough, I didn't have enough information. There were three sizes of eggs: "Large," "Extra Large," and "Jumbo." "Large" was the smallest size. What to do? When my wife told me what kind of eggs to get, was she referring to category or size? I decided that some independent thinking might be risky, and picked up a carton labeled LARGE.

Back at home, Nancy said: "These are cute. Didn't they have any large ones?" I pointed out that in four places and in block letters, the word "Large" appeared on the carton. She said I should have known that by "large" she meant big.

Choosing those eggs was easy compared to what I usually have to do—pick up something for which the only type and quantity description is "some." One evening "some" tinfoil was on the list. At the store, I was directed to a solid wall of foil. Each box, however, was described as containing "aluminum foil," and I asked if they didn't have tinfoil. They didn't. I asked the clerk if he knew of a store that might carry tinfoil. He didn't, but assured me that when people refer to "tinfoil," they really mean "aluminum foil." Having been chewed out for bringing home "Large" eggs when I was told to buy large ones, I was not comfortable with this explanation. My wife may not be a metallurgist, but she certainly knows the difference between tin and aluminum.

There were several brands and sizes. I recognized some of the brands and figured I couldn't go too far wrong there, but had no idea how much to get. The rolls went, in twenty-five-foot increments, from fifteen to two hundred feet in length. Each length came in three different widths. "Some" didn't sound like too much, but I wanted to make sure to get enough. On the other hand, if I appeared with the two-hundred-foot roll, I could be greeted by, "I just wanted to wrap up some food, not build a Quonset hut." As I stared at the stacks of foil, realizing that I was not equipped to make the decision, a mother walked by with a shopping cart and her small children. I decided to rely on her judgment, and asked if she would be good enough to pick a roll of foil, any roll, and hand it to me. "Come along, children" she said without looking at me, and quickened her step.

After getting "a" box of cereal (deciding between "Family" and "Economy" after rejecting "Large"), I picked out "some" chicken, and went home to get my grade.

NOTHING TO EAT

IT seems that every time you turn around, there are new reminders that there is nothing we can eat without causing us physical or emotional harm.

You should avoid beef. Everyone knows that beef is high in cholesterol. Then there's chicken. We used to think we were safe with chicken, as long as it wasn't fried. My wife has a way of cooking pieces of chicken in boiling water so that they end up tasteless, odorless, but, we thought, very healthy. Recently, however, there have been print campaigns graphically describing the conditions under which chickens are raised and dispatched. Anyone with a soul who is exposed to these ads should feel guilty eating chicken. This, however, isn't simply a matter of temporarily enduring an unpleasant emotion. A new study by a team of University of Pennsylvania scientists reveals that anxiety causes white blood cells to cluster just under the skin surface, contributing to such diseases as psoriasis, eczema, and acne. Guilt is a form of anxiety. Chicken, therefore, is bad for the complexion. The same goes for lamb, inasmuch as the quality of a sheep's life, we're told, is no better than that of a chicken. Pigs aren't treated any better. So in addition to boosting your cholesterol level, pork, sausage, and bacon will give you acne.

You should also stay away from fish. Fried fish is obviously bad for you, as it is when it's smoked. Leaving the fish uncooked isn't the answer. There's apparently a parasite in some raw fish that can damage your eyesight.

As for the fish themselves, fatty ones like swordfish have as much cholesterol as red meat. Others, and you're never sure which ones, are loaded with mercury. Catching them yourself doesn't eliminate the risk. At a stream near us, we watch fishermen reel in one shiny trout after another and then throw them back. This, we learned, is not because these people are true sportsmen. Instead, the fish are so full of PCBs that you must disclose having eaten one on an application for life insurance. Fish can also be a source of guilt. I read of one restaurant that stopped serving tuna because dolphins were also being trapped in tuna fishermen's nets. Eat a tuna-fish sandwich and you might as well be killing a dolphin.

You should also avoid fruits and vegetables, impregnated as they are with herbicides, pesticides, rodenticides, fungicides, and chemicals designed to make them easy on the eye and pleasing to the touch. Celery is pretty safe, but since more calories are used up eating it than it has, celery is more properly part of an exercise program than a diet.

You shouldn't drink anything either. Alcohol, of course, is terrible, as are soft drinks, particularly the diet kind. Coffee isn't good for you. Regular coffee has caffeine. Decaffeinated coffee, it was recently reported, will increase someone's low-density lipoprotein, the "bad" cholesterol, by an average of 7 percent.

Dairy products are out. They're high in animal fat and, therefore, cholesterol. With dairy products there's another danger. If the animal was given penicillin or hormones, as is often the case, the cow will have been big and healthy but you've got a problem if you eat what came from it. My doctor also told me to stay away from salt because it raises blood pressure. While I should not have sugar, sugar substitutes are worse.

As for packaged or canned products, you'd have to be crazy to consume them. Based on the list of their ingredients and additives—such as coloring agents, antispoilants, flavoring agents, processing aids, moisture content and acid-alkaline controls—these products seem more likely to have come from Monsanto than the Jolly Green Giant.

When I'm in the grocery store and am supposed to use my discretion, it's comforting to know that agonizing over what to eat is pointless (and unhealthy). It's all bad for me so I might as well pick something that tastes good.

CONGRATULATIONS ON YOUR NEW WASHING MACHINE

MY parents used to tell me that letter writing, as an art, was destroyed by the telephone. One Mother's Day, I came to a different conclusion, and decided that the letter was made obsolete by the greeting card.

I dutifully set out to discharge my Mother's Day obligations and found a card shop with as many aisles as a fair-sized A&P. Above the racks of cards were signs indicating the subject matter of each section. GET WELL was the first one I came to.

In the old days, if your boss was in the hospital, you had to compose a letter dealing with the circumstances along, for example, the following lines:

Dear Chief:
    I hope you are feeling better after that terrible fall. None of us thought that anyone could samba that fast, and being barefoot must have made it all the more difficult. If you

dance again at next year's office party, I hope you'll do it on the floor instead of on top of the Xerox machine.

The doctors, you'll be pleased to learn, predict that your secretary will make a complete recovery.

You don't have to do that anymore. Sprinkled among the cards in each section are tabs indicating subcategories of messages. The employee with the hospitalized boss would first choose between the SERIOUS INJURY and NONSERIOUS INJURY categories. He would then decide on the tone of the message by picking STANDARD, HUMOROUS, or RELIGIOUS. Finally, he would scan the tabs RELATIVE, FRIEND, TEACHER, etc., and find the one for BOSS.

The same is true with birthday cards. Although happy-birthday wishes, in card format, have been around for ages, there is no longer a need to personalize them. Now, that's done at the factory. You find the birthday being celebrated (first, second, etc.), find the tab identifying the type of recipient (NIECE, GODSON, etc.), the kind of message (HUMOROUS or RELIGIOUS) and whether or not the wish is BELATED. There are also tabs for PET, both to and from. You simply select, sign, and send.

The greeting card now provides an alternative to the thank-you note. Searching for the right words to express appreciation is a thing of the past. In the THANK YOU section, you can make your selection from among tabs that read FOR A GOOD JOB, FOR THE BABY GIFT, FOR DINNER, FOR LETTING ME BORROW YOUR SNOWBLOWER, and so on.

I then came across the CONGRATULATIONS section where the categories included NEW CAR, SUCCESSFUL DIET, QUITTING SMOKING, DRIVER'S LICENSE, SCOUTING ACHIEVEMENT, NEW HOME and NEW HOME (RELIGIOUS). Suddenly, I had a terrifying thought. Should I have been sending these things out whenever a friend went on a diet or his kid got another

merit badge? Is that why the dinner invitations seem to
have trailed off?

One part of the store was reserved for cards that did not
recognize a particular occasion but instead were to communicate messages in categories such as LOVING YOU IS FUN,
I'M SORRY, AM I INTERFERING?, IT'S OKAY TO BE YOURSELF, I'M IM-
PRESSED, and IT'S OVER. Behind the tab BECAUSE I'M THE PARENT
the cards were sold out. Why couldn't they have had these
in my bachelor days? Instead of agonizing over how to break
off a doomed relationship, all you have to do now is to
ship off an IT'S OVER card.

I finally found my way to the Mother's Day section. There
were sections for MOM TO MOM, MOTHER-TO-BE, SISTER'S FIRST
MOTHER'S DAY, SINGLE MOTHER, "OTHER" MOTHER, and MOTHER
OF SOMEONE DEAR. There also was a section for WIFE, but the
cards there all had pictures of sunsets and long poems in
script. I ended up making my own.

Part IV

At, or near, the Office

SOMETHING FROM
THE BAR?

AFTER graduating from law school, I began interviewing with firms. I quickly learned that much of the anxiety generated by this profession has little to do with the practice of law.

Law-firm interviews have a standard format—a series of half-hour interviews, followed or preceded by lunch. Lunch is the hardest part. For my first interview lunch, I was taken to a club by a partner and one of his associates. As he put on his reading glasses to look at the menu, the partner asked me, "Something from the bar?'" This was a test, I was sure of it. The question produced terrified indecision. If I said yes, the man would probably write me off as a lush. He himself would have nothing. I pictured him, with arms folded over his chest, looking at me over his reading glasses and glancing periodically at his watch as I drank my beer. On the other hand, if I declined, would he con-

clude that I was not able to function properly in adult social settings?

I asked for a Coke. My host ordered a martini, as did his associate. When the drinks arrived, the waiter left the thick green bottle on the table in front of me lest there be any doubt, to anyone in the place, about who was drinking what.

Then we turned to the menus. Another test, I thought. If I order a thick steak, they'll probably think I'm trying to exploit the firm. If I went with the chicken salad, however, would I come across as lacking self-confidence? I decided on chicken. They both had lobster.

I worked my way through several lunches like that one, learning to deflect questions like "Something to start with?" with "Only if you . . ." or "Not unless you . . ." Apparently, my conduct was passable, for I got some offers. I accepted one, and went to work.

I, like any young associate intent on doing well, strained to produce thorough, imaginative, and typo-free work before the deadline. Obstacles that rose up between me and my objective, such as a typist who tried to talk on the phone and eat a sandwich while doing my work shortly before it was due, with predictable results, turned me into a nervous wreck. I, however, don't think I ever saw anyone as anxious as one of our new lawyers was one day over something that didn't involve his work or a client.

I, at the time, had been a partner for a few years, and was working on a case with a recent law-school graduate. He (Steve) had been with us for only a few weeks, and I was the first person he'd worked for.

Our adversary had sent us a brief with a thick, eight-hundred-page appendix of exhibits. After Steve and I looked it over quickly, I asked him to have a copy made for the client. That was at about 10:00 A.M. I wanted to get to work on the appendix, and when it had not come back from being copied at noon, I called Steve. He checked and told me that they were working on it. That seemed understandable, given the size of the document.

At 2:00 P.M., I asked Steve to check again, and got the same report. I also got the same one at 4:00 P.M. This time I suggested he go to our office-services department and look into it himself. At four-fifteen, Steve appeared at the door to my office. "Ashen" is the only way to describe his look. The delay, he proceeded to explain very slowly, was the result of a mistake he had made in filling out the slip we use to get documents copied. There is a space for the number of copies requested and another one for the number of pages in the document. Steve had put the number of pages in both places.

We both went into the copying room, where we were greeted by the sight of six-feet-high stacks of fresh copies, covering much of the floor in the small room. From behind more stacks, the fellow operating the copying machine, who was visible only from the waist up, gave me a big grin and proudly announced, "Only seventy-five more to go, Mr. Trowbridge."

Within a year, Steve was gone. I wish he'd stayed. After the eight-hundred-copy incident, his work was just about perfect.

MY KINGDOM FOR A NEEDLE AND THREAD

$\mathbf{A}$s occupations go, the practice of law is known as a particularly stressful way to make a living. One of my most hand-wringing experiences, however, took place far from the office and the courtroom.

I was handling a case in which our firm represented a major corporation that had sued the state of New York over a law we believed was unconstitutional. Other companies subject to the same law also sued and soon it was a major piece of litigation, creating real credit problems for the state. In an effort to resolve the dispute, the governor invited the chief executive officers of the companies involved to a meeting. They wanted their lawyers to attend, but the governor refused, finally agreeing to let one lawyer come. I was picked. The meeting was set for nine o'clock in the governor's office downtown. I was to meet my client and the president of the company in front of their building at eight-thirty, and we would drive down together.

I left my apartment in plenty of time that morning, and arrived ten minutes early. As I waited, I reached down to button my suit jacket. The button came off in my hand. Great. Here I was, about to go into the most important meeting of my professional career looking like a bum. I still had ten minutes, though, so I raced the three blocks to a club I belong to where I thought I'd be able to sew it back on. Dashing in, I asked at the front desk if they had a needle and thread. They didn't have one there, and I was directed to the bell captain, who could tell me where the valet was. "Valet," said the bell captain. "That's Mary's operation. You know, it's funny. When you say 'valet,' you automatically think of a man. Mary's been running that place for twelve years now and— Floor? That would be eighteen." The "een" part of the word and I reached the elevator at about the same time.

It was now 8:22. In the elevator, a man got on at the second floor and held the door while asking if I knew where the steam bath was. Tick. Tick. Tick. I didn't. He thought it was four, five, or six, and pushed all three buttons, saying he'd recognize the floor when he saw it. It turned out to be six.

I arrived at the valet at 8:24. It looked deserted. After I called out, a woman (Mary?) came around a partition and asked if she could help me. I blurted out that I'd like to borrow a needle and thread. What color thread? Dark. Black or blue? Blue. Navy okay? Fine. She disappeared behind the partition, and I waited. At 8:27, I walked around the partition to find her raking through a basket of thread. She explained that she was looking for something called button thread. It seems that button thread is much sturdier

than regular thread. She proceeded to make her point by telling me about her son and how she had used button thread to sew buttons on his football pants. He used those things for three seasons, and not one of the buttons even became loose, much less fell off. Now, years later, she's sure those buttons are still on, although she hasn't been able to find the pants lately.

The blood had drained from my face, and I was chewing on the inside of my cheek. Trying not to be rude, I said that any thread would do, and by any, I meant *any*. Any color, any strength. She gave me a funny look, and handed me some blue thread and a needle. It was 8:31. Biting off a foot of thread, I asked if I could take the needle into the elevator with me, figuring that I could reattach the button in the elevator on the way down. She told me that ordinarily she would let me, but the particular needle I had was longer, thicker, or more something than a regular needle, and she only had one left.

I hadn't any words left, and my mouth was probably too dry to get them out anyway, so I sat down to sew. It was 8:34. All is lost, I thought. The client will have given up waiting for me and will have gone ahead to the meeting. I won't be able to find a taxi and will be late for the meeting. The governor won't let me in when I finally get there, because he didn't want me to come in the first place. I've lost the client, that's for sure. The chief executive officers of several of the biggest corporations in the country will tell everyone they know about the experience they had with me and my firm.

At 8:36, the button was on and I was back in the elevator. On twelve I was joined by someone who was trying to find out what floor the library was on and on eight by someone heading for the squash courts. At ground level, I sprinted for the meeting spot and, as I had feared, found the sidewalk deserted. As I started to think about what other careers might be open to me and how much we could get for our apartment, the people I was waiting for walked up. They apologized for keeping me waiting.

The meeting itself was a piece of cake.

THE OZONE
SITUATION

Lᴵᴷᴱ most lawyers, I spend only part of the day practicing
law. Much of my time is taken up by administrative matters
and miscellany such as fighting with our computer system
or deciding how to observe National Secretaries' Day. I
also spend a good deal of time interviewing potential lawyers for our firm. The memory of some of these people is
still with me.

I remember the first applicant I spoke to, some twenty
years ago. Back then the firm's day-to-day hiring efforts were
the responsibility of the most junior associate. On this particular day, that was me. I was busily doing my part to
boost the GNP when the receptionist notified me that an
interviewee had arrived. After introductions, the applicant
handed me his résumé, which revealed a dismal academic
record. He stressed, however, that his grade-point average,
which, as he put it, placed him in the top 95 percent of his
class, was misleading. It did not show how he had im-

proved during law school. To illustrate his progress, he had prepared a chart, which he proceeded to unfold.

The chart was divided into thirds, one for each school year, and graphed the course of his GPA. Across the chart, a bold black line jutted unerringly upward, and would have threatened to pierce the ceiling had his academic career not been cut short by graduation. Upon closer inspection, I noticed an asterisk next to this line, the footnote to which read, "Excluding the following courses: Tax I, Tax II, Constitutional Law, Contracts, Torts, and Property." There was also a barely perceptible dotted line that looked much like the Dow on October 19. It bore the marginal notation, "With Tax I, Tax II, Constitutional Law, Contracts, Torts and Property." He didn't have any references or writing samples, but said I could keep the chart.

I like talking with law students, whose questions make me recall the mysteries law firms held for me years ago, but sometimes I despair of the half-hour interview ever ending. That occurs most often after preliminary banter has been exchanged, the applicant says he has no questions, sits back, and there are twenty-eight minutes left. In such moments, I find myself making comments such as, "My that's an attractive necktie," or "How about those [name of first sports team that comes to mind]!" Often I'll search a résumé frantically for an idea, sometimes wishing I hadn't found one. For example, I well remember the following exchange:

"I note that you worked at the Kit Kat Klub in Los Angeles last summer. What was your position there?"

"Stripper."

"I see. Tell me, what do you make of the ozone situation?"

Equally fresh is my recollection of someone I didn't meet. We had received a letter from a recent law-school graduate in upstate New York who wanted an interview. We answered that we would be pleased to meet with him, and an appointment was set up. An hour after the appointed time, George (we'll call him) still had not appeared, and his wife telephoned. She had driven down with him and asked if he was in our offices. I told her that we were still waiting for him, which was what she had feared. She explained that her husband, enormously talented though he was, had one minor quirk. He was terrified of elevators. We left it that she would look for George and try to send him up.

Another hour went by, and still no George. Again his wife called. George, she reported, was walking around the lobby of our building, trying to find the nerve to make the forty-floor ascent. After describing him, she asked if I would go down to the lobby and interview him there. I said that we really weren't set up to interview that way. I also told her that we like our people to put in an appearance at the workplace from time to time. That apparently would present a problem in George's case, even assuming the ground-floor interview went well.

I never met George, and we didn't hire the stripper. Sometimes, though, when I'm preparing exhibits for a case, I'll get out that chart.

Part V

THE MANNER OF SPEAKING

Remain Comfortably
Seated

THE 1980's are over now, and it's probably not too early to begin characterizing them. If the 1960's were the decade of guilt/conscience and the seventies belonged to the "me" generation, the eighties, I believe, were the era of the euphemism.

I recently read an article about the financial and psychological difficulties of those who find themselves without jobs as a result of corporate downsizing. Downsizing. The word appeared without quotation marks, italics, or a suggestion that it was anything other than a full-fledged and long-standing member of the language. Downsizing (is growth "negative downsizing"?) had quickly and quietly infiltrated the vocabulary, assuming a place alongside words that have been with us since Milton.

I think the airlines started it. A number of years ago, I was trying to get home from the West Coast, and was asked by the ticket agent if a direct flight would be okay. When I tried to find out what that meant, she told me that a "direct" flight was "through." We weren't getting anywhere, but I asked her to ticket me anyway. As it turned out, a crow would have taken a very different route.

At the airport, the posted departure time of my flight was repeatedly pushed back in fifteen-minute increments. The fellow at the counter explained that they were waiting for some "equipment." I thought he meant something like a cotter pin or possibly a wrench. He was talking about the airplane. As we waited, we were instructed to remain "comfortably seated," which I guess meant that we should remove any sharp objects we were sitting on (at that time).

Once we had leveled off in the air, it was announced that we were "free to move about the cabin." I assumed that that announcement was intended for a differently configured airplane. In this one, movement was out of the question. Had they tried to cram in any more seats, the plane would have started popping rivets. Access to either end of the plane was blocked by two fully manned carts wedged into the skinny aisle.

A stewardess then instructed us on certain safety procedures involving life vests and emergency doors equipped with slides. I assumed that this was in case the airplane plummeted from the sky and went crashing into the ocean. I was wrong. This was simply in the event of a "water landing."

Museums soon fastened onto the same technique as a way of dealing with increased costs. Rapidly appreciating artworks were of no help, and any museum tempted to swap an Old Master for cash to fix the leaky roof would have had its institutional head bitten off. "*What!?* You sold the Rembrandt!?" The same transaction sails through unnoticed when described as the "deaccession" of a fine example of the Dutch School.

Then the criminal element caught on, concerned about the negative connotations of terms such as "fraud" and "murder." We now find the mobster, convicted of mincing some of the competition, admitting to "inappropriate" behavior—rather like wearing brown shoes in the evening.

A government official caught with the day's kickbacks in his pocket acknowledges that, like the quarterback who went for the yardage on fourth and three, he committed an "error of judgment." If the crime involves a course of conduct, it is explained as a "judgmental lapse."

It has found its way into the home. My son came home the other day with a new shirt. I asked how much it cost, grabbing the back of a chair for support. He said he would not call it expensive. Instead, it was, as he put it, somewhat "aggressively priced." I did not relax my grip.

AS YOU WON'T RECALL

WHEN our children go back to school each year, I often give thought to what I did and did not learn when I went through the system.

Like anyone with a liberal-arts education, I have had about fifteen years of English. By the time I graduated from college, I could pluck a predicate complement from a crowded page in nothing flat and could distinguish a simile from a metaphor 75 percent of the time. None of that instruction, however, even touched on what I most needed to learn: how grown-ups communicate with each other. Thus, I was let loose in the world without the wherewithal to deal with the broad range of expressions adults commonly use. Take "Let's have lunch someday," for example. My responsive "When?" the first time someone said this to me prompted an inspection for hayseeds behind my ears and an inquiry as to how I liked the big city. How was I supposed to know that that expression means, "This conversation is over now," and no more? No one taught me that the somewhat more emphatic "We *must* get together for lunch" means, "I expect to be tied up for most of the decade."

For those who innocently take these expressions literally, the consequences can be more serious than an embarrassing moment. Woe to the bright-eyed neophyte who takes a heavy felt tip to a draft in response to the apparent invitation, "I have no pride of authorship." Plot a short career path for the employee who puts off something until his "earliest convenience" or who, when told that he "may wish to" do something, decides upon reflection that he doesn't at all wish to and acts accordingly.

It would be easy to work this subject matter into the curriculum. The introductory phrase, for example, could be taught in one brief session. The material is straightforward.

"As you will recall . . ." is used when you believe the listener won't recall what you're about to say. The more forceful "You will remember that . . ." is to be used when you're absolutely certain the listener has forgotten something. If you have to tell someone something he doesn't know, begin your sentence with "As you know . . ."

When dealing with your state of mind, it is important to master the negative. To express an uncomplimentary thought, say you're not saying it. For example, say, "He's stupid" by saying, "I'm not saying he's stupid." By the same token, if you mean to be critical or rude, say you don't mean to be (e.g., "I don't mean to be rude"). When you're sure of something, you must say that you're not entirely sure of the opposite. Thus, if you strongly disagree, say, "I'm not entirely sure I agree."

"Not to belabor the point" is used as an introduction when you're about to belabor a point. If the belaboring will be prolonged, then "Not to prolong the matter" is preferred. When you want to change a conversation's subject, always say, "Not to change the subject." If you're changing from one topic to a completely different one but want a smooth transition, use, "In this connection."

After covering the introductory phrase, students should be ready to tackle the excuse. For example, they should be taught that it is quite unnecessary to own up to the fact that they can't or won't do something. The blame can be laid on an unidentified third party by explaining that one is "not in a position" to do whatever it is. The same technique is useful if one hasn't done something one should have. There's no need to 'fess up. Youth should be taught, as adults have learned, to imply that it's because of the excessive demands of others with the versatile "I haven't had a chance to . . ."

Most important, no matter what you're talking about, use as many words as possible. For example, never say "please call" when "please don't hesitate to call" will do.

It may be, however, that modern educators are better at passing on this information than were teachers in my day. I recently heard my young daughter respond to her younger sister's invitation to join in a game by saying, "I'd love to, but I don't want to."

I'M [NOT] COMING

O<small>NE</small> day I saw a news report on a serious botch by one of the mayor's people. Reporters were jabbing their sharpened pencils at the mayor, pressing for an explanation. At one point, he solemnly said, "I accept full responsibility." The reporters nodded at each other, put away their pencils, and headed for the phones. He, of course, hadn't accepted or done anything. He just wanted to be left alone.

Since then I have thought about the expressions that reflexively roll off our tongues every day, and have come to think that they fall into three categories. In the first are expressions like "I accept full responsibility," which mean nothing. The two other categories consist of expressions whose meaning is the opposite of or different from what the words say.

The purpose of expressions in the first category is to get someone off your back without doing or committing to anything. A particularly effective one is "I'm sorry," as in

"I'm sorry my relentless taunts reduced my sister to tears," or "I'm sorry that isn't covered by your insurance." There is usually as much sorrow in someone who says he's sorry as there is fear in the appliance salesman who is "afraid" your refrigerator will have to be replaced. The emotion involved is similar to that of someone who "regrets any inconvenience."

Another expression that is completely devoid of meaning is often used in our house. To explain this one, by fourth grade we have all learned the parts of speech. Verbs are action words. "Come" is a verb. The phrase "I'm coming," however (or its close commercial cousin, "I'll be right with you") is invariably spoken by someone, in whom no motion is detectable. Just the other day, I made this point to my son, who had been summoned to the dinner table. Long after the words "I'm coming" had left his room, he was still in it. I tracked him down, saying, " 'Come.' Verb. Action word." Gesturing with an index finger, he came back with, "Ah yes, Dad. But a verb can also describe a state of being." "Not this one," I said. "Move." In such moments, I wonder whether education, at least for the young, isn't overrated, but that's another subject.

For some reason, advertising seems to be using this category of expressions more and more, making up new ones all the time. For example, a book will be recommended as a "good read." There is also an ad that describes a beverage as having the virtue of being a "drinking beer." This obviously isn't a disclaimer (no good for cuts or bruises?) any more than the marketing of an automobile as a "road car" warns the purchaser to keep it off fields and pastures. These are not isolated instances. The automobile alone is the source of a number of such expressions. In an apparent appeal to the urban motorist, the vehicle is described as a "street car." For the do-it-yourself type, it is marketed as a "driving machine"; to those who aren't mechanically minded and don't know what is under the hood, it is sold as a "motorcar."

Why, I wonder, is Madison Avenue telling us to buy a book because we can read it, a beer because we can drink it, or an automobile because it can be driven, goes on streets and roads, and has a motor? This use of expressions in the first category may simply reflect the "if-you-can't-say-something-nice" rule we learned as children. It reminds me of my father coaching me on how to react when shown a newborn whose looks do not justify the mother's pride. He told me to say, "That *is* a baby."

In the second category—expressions that mean the opposite of what the words say—members of the love/hate family are heavily represented. "I hate to say it" is invariably spoken by someone who will burst if the words don't come out, and soon. The introduction "We'd love to come over and watch the slides of your trip" never precedes acceptance of the invitation to the viewing.

By far the largest category is expressions whose meaning is simply different from that of the words. For example, "Have a nice day" means, "Whether you live or die is a matter of complete indifference to me." The pseudo-invitation also belongs in this class. "You must come over for dinner" means, "You're still low on our list." Although arguably in this category, "Let's get together" is not; "at your place, if at all" is understood.

Often, the meaning of this kind of expression depends on context. The statement that someone is "unavailable," for example, can mean very different things. When spoken by a child about a father it means, "He is taking a nap"; if the subject is the mother, it means, "She's in the bathroom." When used by a secretary to refer to her recently indicted boss, it can mean either, "He's fled the jurisdiction," or "He's hiding under his desk."

The trick is to place an expression in the right category. Our children, who are approaching adolescence, will have to decide how to categorize "Be careful." We, in turn, will have to decide what to do with "Don't worry."

Part VI

WITH TONGUE IN CHEEK

IN OUR NEXT SEGMENT

I just realized why television is so unsatisfying. Nothing is on. By "nothing," I don't mean nothing good. I mean that rarely is there anything on the screen other than a commercial, a credit, or a preview.

Take, for example, the typical half-hour show. I watched one the other night. It began with lead-in shots of the actors, superimposed over which came, one after another, the name of the writer, producer, director, and a few others. After some commercials, the show began. As I settled in to watch, the words "Cast, In Alphabetical Order" appeared at the bottom of the screen, rolled up to the top, and disappeared. With the action proceeding in the background, name after name moved vertically across the screen. The last name disappeared and just as I was finally able to get an unobstructed view of the show, the word "With" and the name of an actor appeared, followed by "And" with more names. After one more clean shot at the screen, the words "Guest Appearance" appeared with another name. The screen was clear for a few seconds, until someone who would be making a "Special Appearance" was identified. Then it was time for more commercials.

Commercials have their own distractions. Watching them, I often think of the Shakespeare play put on every year by my son's school. This year, as an eighth-grade Lear recited line after line, I nodded off. Several minutes later, I was aroused by the action on the stage and my wife's elbow. Lear was still talking.

By contrast, people in commercials are apparently unable to memorize an 800 number or a phrase longer than "brickface and stucco." Watching television spokesmen, I find myself listing to one side or the other as I try to make eye contact with people who seem to be looking at one of my ears, or either craning my neck or sliding down in my chair as they talk to my forehead or chin.

When the show resumed, it had not been going for long when more names started to appear. As the action continued, names of people with the following responsibilities slowly came and went: Title Sequence, Executive in Charge of Production, Executive Story Editor, Executive Story Consultant, Production Designer, Production Coordinator, Assistant Production Designer, Costume Designer, Assistant Costume Designer, Wardrobe, Makeup, Hair, Technical Director, Lighting Director, Audio, Assistants to the Producers, Associate Producer, Musical Direction, Theme, Stage Managers, Unit Manager, Production Consultant, Executive Consultant, Casting, Original Casting, Post Production Supervisor, Production Associate, and Production Assistant. This crew was for a one-shot, half-hour sitcom—not *War and Peace*. I tried, without success, to get a glimpse of the show between the disappearance of the Executive Story Editor and the appearance of the Post Production Supervisor.

The news is no better. Although the viewer is not treated to the names of all those who had anything to do with the program, the news has something else that cuts into its content just as much—previews. These aren't previews of a show that will be aired that week or a special later in the season, although they have those too. Much of the half hour is consumed by previews of what will take place in that very broadcast.

The news opens with the anchorman summarizing the top stories that will be covered, one of which, like the thirtieth anniversary of the bikini, is calculated to keep you in your seat for the entire half hour. Those previews, however, should have been unnecessary. Part of the immediately preceding local news was devoted to summarizing the stories that will be reported in the upcoming program. The announcements in the local news were themselves unnecessary. The late evening news the day before would have had excerpts of the news stories being worked on for the following day, and the thirtieth anniversary of the bikini would certainly have been featured.

Returning to the national news, after we're told what we'll be seeing, there are some commercials. When they're over, the anchorman only has time to cover a few stories before giving a synopsis and short clips of items he'll cover later. Some will be "in our next segment," with the more interesting stories, like the thirtieth anniversary of the bikini, indeterminately "still to come."

After the next series of commercials and some brief reportage, we're told what will be in the last segment. Early into that segment, we get clips of stories that will be featured on a news and commentary program later that evening. More often than not, some disaster or a fast-breaking political scandal will preempt the thirtieth anniversary of the bikini, or whatever it was that got you to watch the program in the first place.

My wife tells me that this is why a television comes equipped with an "off" button, and one, which she doesn't use, labeled "on."

PERCHANCE
TO DREAM

Returning on a flight from Europe one summer, I saw a report on a breakthrough in the control of jet lag. It seems that researchers have discovered a correlation between jet lag and exposure to light. They have noticed, for example, that when someone shuffles off a plane in Paris after an all-night flight from New York and heads straight to his hotel, he can't sleep because the sun is shining—even though it is three in the morning body-clock time. Scientists, therefore, have experimented with controlling people's exposure to light both before and after crossing time zones, with a noticeable reduction in the dislocations associated with jet lag. One of the researchers who was interviewed cited the case of four men who walked off the plane at Heathrow wearing welders' masks. After being detained for questioning for a short time by airport authorities, they were able to go right to sleep, even though, outside, it was a bright, sunny day.

When it took me two full days to recover from that flight, I decided to find out more about this research. It had been started, I learned, by a Doctor Leitwheyt right here in New York, and he agreed to spend a few minutes with me.

My first question was how he happened upon the relationship between sleep and light. He told me that, like all great discoveries, this one came out of an everyday experience. "Remember Newton and the apple?" he asked. "Same thing." The doctor told me that one night as he was going to bed, he reached out to turn off the light, as he had without thinking for years, and said to himself, "Hey, I wonder what would happen if I left the light on?" He decided to conduct an experiment, and to use himself as the subject. This, he reminded me, was in the tradition of Freud, who psychoanalyzed himself before he turned to other people. The experiment was conducted as follows: The doctor went to bed with the light (100-watt bulb) on. After an hour, he was still wide awake, staring at the ceiling. The doctor usually drops off after being in bed for no more than fifteen minutes, and he therefore concluded that the light was the cause of this behavioral modification.

Leitwheyt didn't stop there. After an hour, the doctor began to reduce the amount of light in the room by substituting less powerful bulbs at regular intervals. During the course of the night, he changed light bulbs every half hour, and stayed awake even though it got increasingly past his bedtime. At about 4:30 A.M., with a 10-watt bulb in the socket, the doctor fell asleep. The following day, he evaluated the data and formulated a conclusion: His ability to get to sleep was due to the 90 percent reduction in wattage. He discounted the fact that he had been up for most of the night and was exhausted from jumping up and down to change light bulbs.

Although the doctor was comfortable with his conclusion, he told me he decided to experiment on a larger sample before releasing his results to the scientific community. He placed ten subjects, all adult males like himself, in two specially designed rooms in his basement. Each room had a one-way mirror, so that he, undetected, could watch the subjects during the experiment. One room had a battery of 150-watt bulbs screwed into ceiling fixtures. The other room had no lights at all. The subjects went into their rooms at midnight. The doctor first observed the subjects in the lighted room and saw that by 3:00 A.M. they were still awake. His attempt to observe the other group was less successful. The doctor told me that, in scientific experiments, it is impossible to anticipate all contingencies. In this case, he had overlooked the fact that a one-way mirror for observing subjects is useless if the room they are in is pitch-black.

At 6:00 A.M., the doctor concluded the experiment. In the lighted room, with the exception of one subject who was curled up facing the wall, everyone was still awake. They were also playing poker. The doctor viewed these results as a .9000 correlation with those of the experiment he had performed on himself.

He opened the door to the other room to find all ten subjects lying on the floor. Some appeared to be unconscious from hitting their heads on the concrete floor after bumping into each other in the dark. The others were asleep. Even if some of the subjects were in fact unconscious, the doctor concluded that for purposes of the experiment, the significant fact was that they were not awake. He therefore made an upward adjustment in the correlation of the results of this experiment to the earlier one, rounding it off to 100 percent.

The doctor told me, in layman's terms, that the implications of his findings for the traveler crossing time zones can be expressed as follows: If you want to go to sleep, find a dark place. If you want to stay awake, turn on a light, preferably a bright one. The doctor has conducted a similar experiment on the effects of noise on sleep, but is reluctant to publish the results until his findings on light have been fully absorbed.

DO I DRINK IT OR ASK IT FOR A DATE?

WE were expecting old friends for dinner, and my wife had bought a cut of beef whose price would have justified giving it space in a display case at Tiffany. I was sent out to pick up a suitable wine for the meal.

After I told the salesman what we were serving, he recommended a particular wine, describing it as "fruity." That sounded pretty good. I like fruit—most fruits, that is. I told him, though, that I'm allergic to coconuts. It's the strangest thing. I first discovered the allergy when I had a piña colada a few months ago, and rolled up my sleeve to show the wine salesman the trace of a rash it had produced on my arm. With this background, I hoped he could understand that I'd have to avoid this wine if it contained any coconut, and asked if he knew whether it did. For some reason, as I was explaining all this, the fellow kept looking at the ceiling. Still looking there, he told me he didn't know. Then I had an idea. Maybe coconut isn't a fruit. Did he

know if it is? He gave out a sigh, which I took to mean "no."

We decided that it would be safer to try something else, and he showed me a very pricey wine that he described as "complex." That wasn't any good either. There is enough complexity in my life already. The last thing I need is to start ingesting it.

The clerk, who was no longer looking at the ceiling but had started tapping his right foot to some beat I couldn't hear, handed me another bottle. This one, he said, was "nicely structured." I held it up to the light, and all I could see was translucent, ruby-colored liquid. This guy's credibility was slipping fast. We then moved to a different part of the store, and he pointed to a bottle that he highly recommended. "Very fleshy," he said proudly. Now, it was starting to get a bit weird. I figured that this wine must be the product of some of that genetic engineering that's been in the news. I told him that I preferred flesh on a plate and not in my glass, thank you very much.

He then suggested describing a few wines and letting me take my pick. One was "big, voluptuous, and seductive"; another was "soft, elegant, and rich"; still another was "young and clean." All in all, though, he preferred one that was "mature and generous, with good body." Something funny was going on. I began to wonder: Is this guy selling wine or running a dating service? I really didn't want to find out. As he continued with "stylish, lightly perfumed, supple . . ." and mumbled something about "nose" and "legs," I slowly backed out of the store.

Once outside, I called my wife, telling her to freeze the meat and whip up some curry. I picked up a six-pack on the way home.